D.R.I.V.E.
The Journey of You

**A How-To Guide to
Overcoming Obstacles,
Discovering Your Purpose &
Pursuing Your Dreams**

Derrick Copeland, Sr.

D.R.I.V.E.: The Journey of You

Copyright © 2024 Derrick Copeland, Sr.

All rights reserved.

No part of this publication may be reproduced or transmitted in any form or by any means electronic or mechanical, including photocopy, recording, or any information storage and retrieval system now known or invented, without permission in writing from the publisher, except by a reviewer who wishes to quote brief passages in connection with a review written for inclusion in a magazine, newspaper, or broadcast.

Print ISBN: 979-8-35094-919-3
eBook ISBN: 979-8-35094-920-9

Cover page designer: Marcus Taylor

Printed in the United States of America

D.R.I.V.E.
The Journey of You

ACKNOWLEDGMENTS

This book has been years in the making; I just didn't know it at the time. The people I've encountered along the way have played a part in some way, shape, or form in not only how I see and process the world around me but how I operate within it. I want to sincerely thank them all for the role they've played in my life. However, there are a few people who I want to point out as special contributors not only to this book but also to my life.

I'd like to dedicate this book to them. To my mother, Catherine Copeland, my first teacher, who has always encouraged me to dream and continually pursue those dreams. Thank you for giving me my very first book to read when I was only five years old. It was *The Power of Positive Thinking* by Norman Vincent Peale. You knew then what the road ahead of me would be like, and you equipped me with something I was going to need to help me through it. Thank you, Momma Rena! I know you're smiling down on me from Heaven.

To my real-life queen, loving wife, and life partner, Yolanda, who supports my dreams and makes me feel like a king in my home. You are my rib. You bring a breath of fresh air into any room you walk into. Other than God himself, you are the most important person in my life. Thank you for everything!

To my godmother, Janice Sweet Fairley, thank you for your unyielding support and encouragement over the years. Thank you for keeping me covered in your prayers all these years. The prayers of the righteous availeth much! May you rest in eternal peace.

To my elementary school principal, Mrs. Mary Snyder (may she rest in peace), who saw something special in me and continued to monitor my growth over the years. To Coach Todd Elliott, my tenth-grade basketball coach. Little did you know that the respect you commanded from your players and the expectations you had for me had a profound effect on me—both then and later in my life. To Godfrey Jones (may he rest in peace). You were my first youth football coach. My first live motivator. You convinced me and a bunch of kids from the 'hood that everything we needed to compete on the field, in the classroom, and in life was lodged deep inside of us. All we had to do was access it. Thank you for teaching me lessons that I carry to this very day.

To all my family, friends, close acquaintances, and associates, past and present: I thank you for playing a part (whether large or small) in my overall development as a person. Finally, and most importantly, I want to dedicate this book to my Lord and Savior, Jesus Christ. Thank you for leading and guiding me with your Holy Spirit through this journey called life. You've truly brought me back to my first love.

TABLE OF CONTENTS

Acknowledgments	vii
Introduction	1
Chapter 1: What Is D.R.I.V.E.?	5
PART 1: Awareness: Where Are You Positioned?	17
Chapter 2: Your Distinction	23
Chapter 3: Your Relationships	39
PART 2: Acknowledgment: Where Are You Going?	51
Chapter 4: Your Inspiration	55
PART 3: Action: How Are You Going to Get There?	81
Chapter 5: Your Vision	83
Chapter 6: Your Evolution	103
Chapter 7: It's Your Time—It's Time to D.R.I.V.E.!	125
About the Author	135
Endnotes	137

INTRODUCTION

What brought me here? How did I get to this point? Those are great questions. Sometimes the answers that we search for our whole lives can be found in the questions that we dare to ask ourselves. I know that has been the case with me. Asking the right questions at the right time had a way of creating the fuel that took me on the journey to seek and discover the answers. Along the way, it helped to form and shape me in a way that brought three factors into full view. Those were awareness, acknowledgment, and action. These factors became a constant consideration in every major endeavor or experience that I came across. They helped me determine if I would stay where I was, if I would move forward, and which direction I would take. I will talk about them more in this book, and my hope is that these will serve as guardrails to help keep you on the road, moving forward, and heading in the direction that will take you to your desired destination in life.

On the flip side of asking the right questions at the right time is choosing not to ask the questions at all. Though we can certainly do this, when we choose not to ask, then we remove ourselves from a journey that could otherwise have fulfilled a longing that we've held but never ventured to travel.

This book will take you on a journey to create *awareness* (in Part 1), evoke *acknowledgment* (in Part 2), and motivate you to take *action* (in Part 3) in your specific endeavor. As you read this book, my hope is that you will see themes and concepts to provide you the energetic fuel to seek and discover your own "aha" moments. These moments can help to transform your life for the better as you travel on a road that is undeniably your own.

Another hope of this book is to help you realize, or solidify, who you are and who you were created to become. I want to touch your heart to help you move further along your journey to realize your purpose, potential, and destiny. This book is the result of a promise that I made to God many years ago that if He would do something which I considered to be extraordinary in my life (a modern-day miracle), I would do whatever He prompts me to do, no matter the cost. This book is a realization of that promise, and my intent is that all who read this book will be blessed beyond measure. Chains will be broken, and things that were once seen as obstacles are now seen as opportunities. Thank you, God, for giving me the inspiration to write this book.

Throughout this book, I will share insights and lessons I have learned from the people, places, and things that have impacted me in a significant way along my life's journey over the years. I will refer to these insightful lessons as "markers." Think of the last time to you took a road trip and happened to notice the mile marker on the side of the highway. Interstate mile markers are the vertical green signs on the edge of highways placed at one-mile intervals. They show the number of miles from where the interstate route entered the state. The numbering always begins at the southern state line on north–south routes and at the western state line on the east–west routes. This can help you determine which direction you're going and how far you are from a border. Just as it is important to be aware of mile markers when you're traveling in your automobile, it is equally important to acknowledge mile markers in your life because it reminds you of how far you've come already and of the movement that has brought you to this point. Whenever you enter a new state, it's important to be mindful of the rules and requirements of that state—like the speed limit, if there are tolls, and the geographical landscape and terrain. Why? Because this will help you make the necessary adjustments to be fully operable without your movement being inhibited.

Just as if you're traveling along a physical highway and you notice a mile marker, I will occasionally, throughout the book, post a "Spiritual Marker" to provide insights and reflect on the portion of my spiritual journey that helped me crystallize some life lessons to gain a clearer perspective. Whether you have the same spiritual beliefs or different ones, there are very practical and impactful strategies throughout the book that you can leverage to use in your life in ways that can benefit you.

Just by virtue of living, I can imagine that you have encountered obstacles. Some obstacles you may have gotten around; others you may still be trying to figure out how to handle. So keep reading. Find those things that resonate most with you. This book is packed with many lessons and strategies that can save you time from having to journey down every road. *Road trips are good, but a trip with a roadmap can be even better.*

The journey of life is filled with different landscapes at different points in our lives. There will be some mountains, some valleys, some flatlands, some wet spaces, and some dry patches. I have learned through this journey that everything (good, bad, or otherwise) can be used to equip us for each stage and season of our lives. It is vitally important that we remember this, because if we don't, we will lose hope while we're on the journey and give up or just travel aimlessly in a direction that takes us nowhere. To understand why I have the outlook I have, we will look back at my journey. It is a journey filled with many joys, mixed in with heaping doses of sadness, confusion, and frustration. A journey filled with hope for the future, but anxiety over how that future would come to be my present.

The goal of this book is to:

- provide you with the tools and strategies to overcome obstacles in your life, and
- equip you with the skills to discover your purpose and pursue your dreams.

So, just sit back, buckle up your seat belt, and let's go for a ride.

Chapter 1: What Is D.R.I.V.E.?

DRIVE (*v*): "to operate and control the direction and speed of a motor vehicle" (Merriam-Webster)

> **"Attitude drives actions. Actions drive results. Results drive lifestyle."** —Jim Rohn

I remember visiting a new city for the first time, and while there my family and I went to an amusement park. This park happened to be one that I had never visited before. One of the first things I made sure to do when we showed our tickets to the attendant was to visit the big sign located just inside the gate that showed a large map of the park, with everything from rides to shows to food spots, right on down to restrooms. But even more important than any of those destinations was a big red dot that read, "You Are Here!" This point on the map let me know specifically where I was in relation to where I wanted to go. That proved to be a crucial move, because in order to know where I'm going, I must know where I'm currently positioned.

This is the basis of this book. D.R.I.V.E. is about discovering where you are, where you're going, and how you're going to get there. Not only that, it will address the question of what is going to drive you to get to your desired destination. Will it be excitement for the future, will it be hurt from the past, or better yet, will it be a wish without wings? Whatever it may be, D.R.I.V.E. will help you consider the questions that lead to the specific answers in your own journey as you navigate your life—whether that be personally, professionally, relationally, spiritually, or emotionally.

The stories we tell ourselves contribute to what drives us. How does that come to be, and why do we tell ourselves "stories"? Our experiences in life, both good and bad, have a deep effect and influence on us. Sometimes we may tell ourselves stories to ease the pain of an experience, or maybe it's easier to believe what someone else has told us many times or many years back. The thing about experiences is that you can't "un-experience" them (if there is such a word) and delete them from your past. Nor can you "copy and paste" your most positive experiences and make them your present-day reality. These notions led me to ask myself what story I am telling myself, good or bad. I didn't know it when I began this journey, but I had to find out what was driving my life.

Everyone has a story. Everyone has something that's driving them to something, to help them make it through challenging times. But is whatever is driving you sustainable? Can it stand the test of time? If it cannot, what is the result when it runs out? You owe it to yourself and to those who are important to you to heed the navigational instructions that ultimately lead you to your destination.

Embrace your story. Tell the truth to yourself about your story. But be hopeful and know that your story is still in the making. It's still being written. You have the power to affect those chapters with the Who, the What, the When, the Where, and the How.

I came to understand that we are all uniquely qualified to tell our stories and to travel our individual paths. We uniquely have our own strengths, pain, experiences, and passions. Considering that, we are uniquely qualified to live out our own individual stories, and the world is waiting to hear them.

For the purposes of this book and the D.R.I.V.E. concept, we are each the vehicle, while our life's journey is the road, and movement (in its proper season) is the goal. The components of D.R.I.V.E. become the fuel that moves us from one point to the next.

D.R.I.V.E. examines what I call the Five Gears of Operation. Those gears are:

- Your **Distinction** (recognizing, understanding, and valuing who you are and your unique qualities)
- Your **Relationships** (recognizing and understanding how your interpersonal connections impact your journey's trajectory, potential, and sustainability)

- Your **Inspiration** (recognizing, understanding, and maximizing your passion, which leads to your purpose)
- Your **Vision** (ability to see something, not just as it is today but what it has the potential to become)
- Your **Evolution** (displaying the willingness and courage to change, grow, and develop to a greater form of yourself)

D.R.I.V.E. is designed to help give your life structure and a navigational route as you take your journey. You will be aligned to move in the direction of those things that are important to you to accomplish more in your life, your relationships, your organization, or whatever it may be. These three essential questions address internal forces that drive us down various paths:

1. Where am I currently positioned in life?
2. In what direction is my life moving?
3. How do I get to my desired destination?

You will learn concepts to identify potential obstacles that threaten, delay, or even halt your journey and be introduced to the 3A Method to counteract those obstacles. The components of the 3A Method are:

1) **Awareness**: your distinction and your relationships

2) **Acknowledgment**: your inspiration

3) **Action**: your vision and your evolution

This method can help you see obstacles as opportunities waiting to happen. It is also meant to build you up from the inside out and to help you see yourself from a new perspective. When you SEE yourself the way you were created to be, you can BE who you were created to be, and DO what you were created to do!

My Story
MY WINDSHIELD MOMENT
The Event: 12/12/84 (A Day That Will Live in Infamy)

On December 7, 1941, at about 8 a.m., Japanese planes filled the sky over Pearl Harbor, Hawaii. Bombs and bullets rained onto the vessels below. At approximately 8:10, an 1,800-pound bomb smashed through the deck of the battleship USS *Arizona* and landed in its forward ammunition magazine. The ship exploded and sank with more than 1,000 men trapped inside. Next, torpedoes pierced the shell of the battleship USS *Oklahoma*. With 400 sailors aboard, the *Oklahoma* lost her balance, rolled onto her side, and slipped underwater. President Franklin Delano Roosevelt (FDR) termed it a "day that will live in infamy."

My Pearl Harbor moment came on December 12, 1984. It was a day that I will never forget. I call it my Day of Infamy. I was fifteen years old. It was just a normal day during basketball season, and I was at basketball practice at school. I was a sophomore in high school and was warming up and shooting before the coach started practice. As we were shooting around, my older brother walked into the gym and told my coach he needed to talk to me, so I got my stuff and went out to his car. It was wintertime in Michigan, so it was snowing outside. On this cold, damp, overcast day, I could hear the windshield wiper blades intermittently rotating back and forth every few seconds. We didn't drive anywhere; my brother simply leaned back in his seat and stared out the front windshield, clearly measuring his words and carefully thinking of what he was going to say. He finally proceeded to tell me that the person whose last name I bear was not my father. He was telling me this because later in the week

I would have to take a blood test to determine whether this person was my biological father. My brother wanted to spare me the inevitable surprise that I would face, but in doing so, he unloaded a bomb on me.

Just like the USS *Oklahoma* and the USS *Arizona*, I was surprise-attacked, air raided, torpedoed, and sunk. As I sat there in the car, it was like time was frozen. I was literally suspended in time. As the weight of the reality that he shared with me began to ooze its way into the consciousness of my mind, I could hear the rhythmic sound of the windshield wipers getting slower and slower . . . fainter and fainter . . . until finally, it stopped . . . and time, as I knew it, stood still. After what seemed like a four-hour conversation but was more like a thirty-minute one, I composed myself, wiped away my tears, got out of the car, and walked past my teammates and coaches who were practicing and into the locker room. I collected my clothes out of the locker and brought them back to the car. When I went back to practice the next day, as I was entering the court, my coach asked me if I was alright. I said yes. And from that point on, I began to learn the art of compartmentalization. I didn't have to learn how to compartmentalize; it was just a natural coping response to deal with that situation. Though that conversation in the car was relatively short in length, its effects were long-lasting.

Most of us have had such a day. A day, a moment, a period that deeply affects or alters the trajectory of our lives. A day when time stands still. A day that shifts your life into a certain gear and sends you searching for answers.

Just as the Pearl Harbor surprise attack awoke a sleeping giant, causing the United States to build itself into what would become a world superpower, my day of infamy awoke something in me that would cause me to accept the challenge that was before me to become better, not bitter. The aftermath of that day is what would DRIVE me to begin the process of asking the important questions that my journey's path would ultimately answer.

They say the two most important days in a person's life are the day they are born and the day they find out why. Well, for me, it's slightly different. The two most important days of my life were the day I was born and the day I *asked the question* why I was born. You see, there are levels to this. It wasn't just the fact that I was asking the question of why I was born; it was also *whom* I was asking. I was asking God to reveal to me why I was born. Even as I write this, I find some emotion rising up from the pit of my stomach, because I vividly remember how broken into pieces I was. But even in that broken, deflated, lost, and sunken place that I was in, I gathered up the courage to ask the question, "God, if you are who you say you are, then why was I even born in the first place?" If *this* was the result of being born, to receive this revelation at *this* point and time in my life, then what was the point of being born in the first place? Because I didn't know who I was!

I felt broken to the depths of my soul. I felt wounded. I didn't have the answers, and I felt that I had come "to the end of myself." This allowed me to come to a place of humility. I turned to my faith with many questions. I had heard that God would be near and keep me close[1], but I needed rest and peace for my soul, because my pain went down into my soul.

There are times when I look back and my heart weeps for that fifteen-year-old kid trying his humanly best to be strong in a situation that he didn't create. The truth has been revealed to him in a way that totally catches him off guard, and he finds himself lost. It's like being a cast member in a school play. You're on stage and playing out the role that has been assigned to you, and the backdrop is something familiar to you. However, later in the same scene, you're still playing your role, but you turn around and the entire background has changed, and you ask yourself, "Where am I?" It has you wondering what was really going on the whole time you were on stage playing your part, but with limited information.

Whenever there's a trauma, there is going to be something that dies and will never come back to its original form. But then, in a very divine way, the remaining pieces can be put back together, and our lives can be even better than we ever imagined. Is it difficult? Yes. Will it take time? Yes. Will you feel like giving up? Yes. However, the work you do to get beyond the thing that got you stuck or slowed down can be the very thing that helps you to navigate and head toward the things you want and value in life. You may ask yourself, "Are *true* happiness and joy really on the other side of that pain?" I'm here to tell you that they are! I wouldn't be attesting to this if it were not true. You see, my personal journey caused me to have tough conversations with myself, others, and my God. I said to God that if he's real, then he's got to show me. Because I can't live my life off what someone else's experience of God is. I needed to have my own experience, and I needed him to show himself to me.

Even though in my heart of hearts I kind of knew that the man I called father wasn't my father—I mean, he had a very dark complexion, and I had a light complexion, and we looked nothing alike—but even with that, I never allowed myself to think that I didn't have a father. Even though this person was very distant from me in terms of a relationship, it was still something—this was still someone I could look at and say that we shared the last name. And no matter how little contact he had with me, he was still my father. My brother's announcement to me felt like someone violently stuck a sharp pitchfork into my stomach, rotated it 180 degrees, and pulled it out. I was literally devastated! I was hurt beyond measure. There was no scale accurate enough to measure the level of pain that I felt. If the pain wasn't bad enough, it put me in a place where I felt alone. I felt abandoned. All I could do at that time was cry. The only thing that was in my heart was heartache and pain. I had never felt like that before in my life and haven't felt like that since then. At fifteen years old, I didn't have the wherewithal to do anything that could change my situation. I was just stuck with my feelings, and I was forced to deal with them.

When I think back on that day, I still get chills because I know the depths of raw pain and emotions that I experienced that day and in the days, months, and years that followed. In the same way that news devastated me as a fifteen-year-old young man, I'm also very amazed at how over all these years, and despite the ramifications that news like that could bring (especially during that critical period in my life), it prompted me to action. That experience, looking back in hindsight, is what spurred on the questions that ultimately led me to D.R.I.V.E. Those questions were: How does my DISTINCTION affect me? How do my RELATIONSHIPS affect my trajectory? Then eventually, where does my INSPIRATION come from? And once I have it, what VISION do I have for myself? Finally, how do I EVOLVE to achieve all of this?

I was at a "moment of belief." This was my personal fork in the road in which I ultimately had to decide what I believed about myself, others, and even God. Little did I know at the time that I would come to several moments of belief at different points and times in my life. These points would ultimately determine whether I would continue with the process or go my own way based on emotions, pain, and unforgiveness and miss out on what was purposed for my life.

The days, weeks, months, and eventually, years, that would follow would be bittersweet. Life was continuing to move on, and I was continuing to achieve some of the goals that I had set for myself, both scholastically and athletically. Yet even with milestones being achieved, there was also a sense of loss. A sense of "what if." A sense of "what do I do now?" Because I had no basis for how to handle certain things in my life, I had to learn on the fly. Things like standing up when you shake someone's hand, and have a firm handshake. Look them in the eyes when you talk to them. Speak up when you're talking. Things that I envisioned a father teaching his son. Over the years I learned how to "get by." I was a pro at describing my father when someone would ask me about him. I would say that he lives in Detroit and that he works at Ford Motor Company. I mean, heck, that seemed like an appropriate thing to say—even if it weren't true. The pain of the truth was too much to verbalize to myself, much less having to explain to someone, "Well, you see, I really don't know who my father is. It's kind of complicated, you know?" Rather than go through that uncomfortable and painful explanation that even I did not understand, I would give my canned and brief answer: "He lives in Detroit, works at Ford. He and my mom divorced when I was young." I would then move from that convenient tale to the next subject like an award-winning actor transitioning into the next scene.

I didn't know who I was. What was really my last name? Who was I? Personally, I looked to my faith to help me answer these questions, and in the years to follow I mustered the courage to initiate the crucial conversations and ask the tough questions to get the answers I needed from the people I needed them from. I remember learning that I was created by God and called by name[2]. I really needed that. I needed to know that someone *saw* me and was *calling* me by my name and would be with me wherever I go[3].

In retrospect, the worst day in my life was actually the best day of my life. I found guidance and direction that kept me going, and I'm still here. Still kicking. Still thriving. Still in awe at how such a traumatic, yet pivotal time in my life could set me on a path to learn how to navigate this journey called life.

CONSIDER and ASK YOURSELF:

- Most of us have a "day of infamy" where it feels like time stands still and it shifts our life into a certain gear and sends us searching for answers.
    - » Identify that day in your life. What was that moment for you?
- There are times in our lives—our "moments of belief"—where we will come to a personal fork in the road in which we'll have to consider what we believe about ourselves and our lives. These points ultimately determine if we will continue with the process that we are in or go our own way based on emotions, pain, and unforgiveness and miss out on what was purposed for our life.

- » What was your "moment of belief," and how did it affect how you viewed the world?
- » How did it affect how you viewed yourself?

- Life continues to move on, and we can achieve goals and even milestones while feeling a sense of loss—a sense of "what if," a sense of "what do I do now?"—because we are not sure how to handle certain things in our life.
  - » Are you living out your life in a way that you're satisfied with?
  - » What could you do differently to live out your life in a way that that satisfies you?

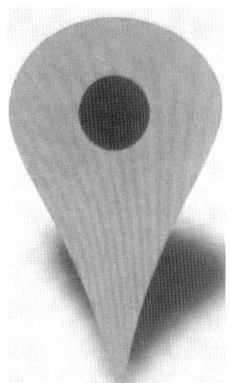

PART 1: Awareness: Where Are You Positioned?

"Self-awareness gives you the capacity to learn from your mistakes as well as your successes. It enables you to keep growing."
—Lawrence Bossidy

As driven and ambitious as we may be, we're consistently on the move, and though there may be things internally, even in our past, that create a weight for us, we sometimes push them down or sweep them under the rug and keep moving so they don't "slow us down." This book will help create awareness and help leverage any personal obstacles that may hinder you from being a better version of yourself. It's meant to help you gauge what's driving you and determine the direction it's taking you.

Self-awareness is knowing yourself and how others see you. It is about understanding who you are, what drives you, your goals, and your aspirations. There are two types of awareness I want to probe, internal self-awareness and external self-awareness. I call this the "inside out approach." The thought here is that what starts out inward ultimately works itself outward. Internal self-awareness focuses on those things that we think and feel about ourselves. It involves knowing our strengths and weaknesses, as well as what we value or find important in our lives. External self-awareness is being tuned into how others perceive us. The two types of self-awareness are equally important. Here are some reasons why:

1. **We will better know ourselves.** Whether it's a personal or professional introduction, one of the first questions asked is "Tell me about yourself." Our ability to know and comprehend who we are, how we think, what we value, and the goals we strive to achieve are all or in part dependent on our comprehension of ourselves.

2. **We will better identify and comprehend our strengths and weaknesses.** This is a critical aspect of self-awareness because knowing and understanding our strengths and weaknesses makes us better equipped to take on life's opportunities and challenges. When we take the necessary time and effort to identify our strengths, we can then be vigilant and intentional in maximizing them. Similarly, once we've taken the time to honestly identify and comprehend our weaknesses, being honest with ourselves and patient (knowing that life is a marathon, not a sprint), we can work to improve them over time.

3. **We will improve our problem-solving skills.** This is the process of finding solutions to difficult or complex issues and analyzing information from an objective perspective. Whether personal or professional, this is a very useful ability in many situations. When you're self-aware, you are able to identify the subjective parts of yourself, like your feelings and opinions, and do your best to not let them play too big of a role in your problem solving.

4. **We will improve our ability to make sound decisions.** This is a hugely important life skill that should not be taken lightly. Among other common traits, great decision makers tend to be proactive, fact-oriented, open-minded, and confident. They take the time to assess their own thoughts and feelings inwardly before working outward. Identifying and understanding your strengths and weaknesses can be very powerful tools to lead you to a decision that best fits your situation.

A lack of awareness has the potential to create a false narrative, where someone has the potential to operate in non-reality at times, even when they get feedback from others indicating areas of concern. Knowing who we are and how others see us builds the foundation for being highly effective, making intelligent decisions, and forging meaningful relationships.

When someone lacks self-awareness, they're unaware of their own impact on others and the world around them. Here are a few traits of someone who lacks self-awareness:

1. **They have no tact.** Though there are times when being direct or even blunt is necessary, it pays to know when to speak freely and when to use tactful, measured words. If

you find yourself frequently expressing things that annoy or upset people, it's likely you lack self-awareness. It's important to be able to read a room and know when it's appropriate to share certain thoughts or opinions.

2. **They are overly sensitive to constructive feedback, even when it's meant to help.** Constructive feedback is meant to address weaknesses, develop skills, improve performance and further one's growth. It is important for us to be able to take both positive and negative feedback well. If someone gets defensive or totally ignores advice about something they could improve on, that could be an indication that they lack self-awareness.

3. **They feel they're always right** and can do no wrong. You may be blind to your own flaws if you don't acknowledge other perspectives or accept your own mistakes. If you have trouble seeing things from other viewpoints, then you're unaware of your own weaknesses. If we're unable or even unwilling to see others' points of view, it's likely because we're not aware of our own shortcomings and lack the ability to step back and see situations in an objective manner.

4. **They have no idea what their strengths and weaknesses are.** Because self-awareness is an essential component to personal growth, it benefits us to know what our weaknesses are so we can work on improving them. And if we're not aware of our strengths, we may not be maximizing them to our full capacity. We may subsequently miss out on valuable experiences and opportunities that could otherwise be afforded to us.

What to Do If You Lack Self-Awareness

If, after some self-reflection, you realize you lack in the self-awareness department and would like to change this—that's awesome! The biggest hurdle has been completed. Here's some things you can do to become more self-aware:

1. **Keep a journal.** This is something that I have personally done for years. Writing down my thoughts and feelings helped me to understand them better. I've also been able to look back over my past entries to see how my thoughts and feelings on certain things have either changed or stayed the same over the years. Doing this can help you see how certain patterns (either good or bad) have developed over time.

2. **Spend time alone.** This will allow you to focus on your own thoughts and feelings. Though this may be difficult for those who are used to being around others all the time, it's very helpful to make some time for yourself for self-reflection.

3. **Observe your behavior.** One way to become more self-aware is to simply observe your own behavior. Keep in mind those things that you do and say, and how they make you feel. Also, think about why you do the things that you do and whether you're happy with them. If there's a part of your behavior you're not happy with, acknowledge it and try to change it.

4. **Talk to other people.** Talking to others about how they think and feel may help you understand your own emotions a little better, while at the same time helping you see things from another person's perspective. It can also help to talk to people you trust about your own work on self-awareness and ask for their honest feedback. This can help you

become more accepting of feedback while also providing great insight on how others perceive you.

5. **Be honest with yourself.** This is probably the most important of them all. If you want to become more self-aware, being honest with yourself is crucial. Don't try to ignore your negative thoughts or emotions, as this has the potential to only make them worse. Acknowledging that you have negative thoughts and feelings is an important part in becoming more self-aware. Once you've identified and acknowledged to yourself that you have them, then you can start to work on changing them.

Though becoming more self-aware takes time and effort, the resulting benefits are well worth the investment. It can improve your relationships, help you understand yourself better, and lead to a higher level of personal satisfaction.

So if you're lacking in self-awareness, don't fret! Self-awareness, just like a muscle in your body, can be exercised, strengthened, and developed.

Chapter 2: Your Distinction

Distinction (*n*): "a difference or contrast between similar things or people"; "excellence that sets someone or something apart from others" (Merriam-Webster)

"The most precious jewels are not made of stone, but of flesh."
—Robert Ludlum

Great things are on the horizon, and it starts with YOU! It starts with you recognizing, understanding, and valuing who you are and your unique qualities. I believe when God made you, he broke the mold. You are a masterpiece. A one in a 108 billion work of art. The estimated number of people who have ever lived on Earth is 108 billion. Out of all those billions of people, not ONE of them was or is exactly like you. You are a crown jewel who has value. When we understand and appreciate who we are and what makes us unique, we can then do what inspires and empowers us.

Even though we are as distinct as the rarest jewel in the world, there is a fundamental question that we often ask ourselves at different points and times in our lives, and that question is simply, *"Who Am I?"* It is a question that is oftentimes tied up in what we do for a living, where we live, who we're born to, what we have, or what we don't have. As elementary as it may seem, none of these things determines who we are. They only determine the circumstances by which we were born and what we may or may not have attained in this world in our years of living.

Celebrated author, speaker, and coach Tony Robbins has often said, "Your identity is the strongest force in the human personality[4]." Everything you can do and everything you cannot do is directly related to your identity. Simply put, it's what you believe about yourself that determines whether your identity will take root and grow or whether it will become dormant. Your identity is something that must be recognized for it to grow. To further show this, psychologists conducting the self-recognition test[5] asked children, "Who's in the mirror?" At eighteen months or younger, children don't usually associate themselves with the image in the mirror. But as kids grow, they can understand they're looking at themselves. Self-recognition (knowing and understanding who you are) is an important mark of healthy growth and maturation.

When you understand your uniqueness and have a true appreciation for it, you can grab hold of the fact that you have unique abilities, skills, and gifts that have been assigned to you. Because of this assignment, nobody can exercise your gift like you—that's your unique quality. *True to your unique quality is the fact that there is absolutely no reason you should desire to be someone else.* It's as if you're telling the Creator (God) himself that you're not happy with what he created. It's like someone giving you a gift that they took the time to craft by hand with detailed specifications, and you look it over and say, "Mmm, nah, I'd rather have something else." Consider these points:

1. You *can't* be someone else, no matter how hard you may try.
2. You could end up wasting valuable time and energy that can be used to cultivate and improve yourself to be a better *you* that you can be.
3. Finally, there's no feeling in the world like discovering and building on your own talents and abilities *and* appreciating who you are and what you have in the process.

One of the first ways I learned about how my identity was shaped was from my youth league football coach back in my hometown of Jackson, Michigan. His name was Godfrey Jones. He was a college-educated man who played football during his collegiate years. When I knew him, he coached a team of kids who were from the "other side of the tracks," meaning less fortunate. Many of us came from single-parent households, so seeing a strong man with a commanding presence on a daily basis was a confidence booster right there. In addition, this was a man who was very encouraging, yet demanded nothing less than our very best effort, both on the football field and in the classroom. When he wanted us to know who we were, compared to other more fortunate individuals, he would say things like, "They put their pants on just like you do, one leg at a time." He knew that if we could see ourselves in a certain way, then it would affect our behavior and even the outcome of the game. But I was pleased that even beyond a football game, that way of thinking would stay with us, guiding and influencing our behavior well into our adulthood. Considering in hindsight where we came from, including how "disadvantaged" our situations may have appeared, I now understand that was not our condition but our conditioning. What mattered was where we took those things that were viewed as obstacles and converted them into opportunities. So, remember, what appears to be a bad situation or misfortune is not your condition, it's your conditioning. It becomes an opportunity to work through that situation to strengthen yourself and be better because of it.

You were created with purpose. You were born on this earth and have a purpose. Regardless of the circumstances that brought you into being, you were born. That was not an accident. You were meant to be here, and you have something to offer the world that you can uniquely bring. When you know your worth, you don't settle for less. We're living in a day where there's so much opportunity to compare ourselves to others. With all the social media that's out there (Facebook, Instagram, Snapchat, Twitter, etc.), we're continually exposed to flashy highlights of people's lives. You don't typically see the "doom and gloom" or "valley" experience of someone's life. It's usually the "mountaintop" experiences that we see and that we willfully share for others to see. Considering all of this, it can be easy to fall into the trap of not appreciating who *you* are and what *you* bring to the table because your focus is on the "highlights" of others (that may or may not be reality).

Because you are a unique and special creation[6], that alone is reason to shout! We each have gifts and treasures inside every one of us. It's our duty to search and find what those gifts are. That shouldn't be that hard to find. Usually those are tied to what we're naturally inclined to do and what we're good at without much effort. It's also tied to what others say we do quite well. We talk about this in more detail later in the book. We *are* valuable, and that value goes beyond our possessions and is innately tied to the gems and purpose within us. If our value is in our job, our kids, our appearance, our spouse, then what happens if any of those things is no longer with us? Does our identity and who we are go right along with it? I hope not.

SPIRITUAL MARKER: I've personally found that the only thing that can keep me when all else is stripped from me is the One who needs no one or nothing outside of itself to survive. The One who has all power within himself and who loves me. The One who is the giver of life.

When you believe in yourself, you're telling the world "Watch out—here I come!" You're making a declaration that you're going somewhere, and that has a powerful effect on others! It draws others to you. Everybody wants to be associated with someone who's going somewhere! It's inevitable. When you *know* who you are, *embrace* who you are, and walk with confidence, you shine a light that illuminates beyond you! But that never happens if you don't know who you are. To know who you are you must go back to the One that made you—the Almighty God! You have his stamp of approval built into your DNA.

Your identity plays a profound role in shaping your actions and choices. It serves as the compass that steers us toward our purpose and potential. You must know who you are in order to do what you were purposed to do.

When this finally became real in my life, it was like the Red Sea opened up for me. Like I was a running back, running through a gaping hole with nothing but open field in sight. I was able to navigate my life's journey with a little more clarity and authenticity.

To become the better version of yourself, you must believe in yourself. Create a routine to recite positive statements and affirmations out loud. You need to renew your mind daily[7] because hard days will come and doubt will arise, so you have to expect it and be prepared to counteract it. I purposely stop short of saying "become the *best* version of yourself" because if breath is in our lungs and we are fortunate enough to live another day, the opportunity to "better our best" is always present.

Remember, whatever you feed, your mind will grow! If your mind is full of critical thoughts of yourself, then that's how you'll see the world—through the lens of always critiquing and minimizing yourself, never quite measuring up. But if you fill your mind with positive words and thoughts of yourself, and if you place yourself in positive environments, then that will manifest through you. To the extent that you can control it, it is up to you to be in an environment where your mind can be nurtured. If there are circumstances beyond your control where a positive, nurturing environment cannot be accomplished, consider these tips on how to stay positive anyhow:

1. Take time for yourself.
2. Be the change you want to see.
3. Identify the source of negativity and move away from it.

4. Learn to enjoy life, one day at a time. (Embrace trying and learning new things. Don't allow fear or worry about the future to keep you from living fully today.)

5. Write down three things you are grateful for and revisit it every day without fail. (This will help you stay positive because they remind you of the person you are and the good things happening in your life anyway.)

6. Don't let others take away your sense of hope. If you find yourself in a negative environment, seek professional guidance or guidance from a trusted individual who has demonstrated integrity and a history of making good decisions.

Again, *whatever you feed, your mind will grow. Whatever you starve, your mind will shrink*. It can be conditioned to do whatever you direct it to do. Positive thoughts and affirmations (and the belief in those positive thoughts and affirmations for yourself) can make the difference between you making your dreams come true and you living below your potential. This is an essential starting point. The conversation that you have with yourself is everything! *What story are you telling yourself?* You ultimately become who you think you are in your mind and subsequently what your actions reinforce. If you tell yourself you're not good enough, you're not worthy enough, you don't deserve the best that life has to offer, then guess what—you won't get the best that life has to offer you because you're not going to look for it. Ultimately, *the way you see yourself on the inside will manifest itself on the outside.*

When you're on the road to self-improvement, it's important to know who you are and what you bring to the table. See yourself through the lens of the best-scenario version of you. See yourself accomplishing that goal, setting that record, winning that competition, getting that dream job, or becoming a successful entrepreneur. Tell yourself you can do it! Start your day by expressing gratitude for waking up and having another opportunity to work toward becoming even better.

Give yourself permission to be great! Never shrink yourself to fit in to someone else's view of you. Create room for your dream. In time, your dream will create room for you.

Who Am I?

Who you are is more important than what you do. Now I know this seems like a pretty vague blanket statement, so let me take the time to clarify. When you know who you are, it affects what you do. What you *do* is largely influenced by what you think of yourself and the actions that can follow. This is important because what you're doing can change, and the circumstances surrounding that can change, and when that happens, you're left with who you are. Then the question becomes, is that enough? Will you be able to live with yourself (outside of what you do)? This is played out in so many of life's scenarios. The once accomplished and celebrated athlete now struggles to find out who they are once an unexpected injury ends their promising career. Maybe it's the long-tenured employee who took pride in being the subject matter expert in their field and now finds themselves on the receiving end of a job termination due to company cutbacks. Whatever the scenario, life, at some point or another, will remove those things that we sometimes hide behind and will subsequently require us to come face-to-face with the question, "Who am I?" *True success happens from the inside and works its way outside.*

Be very careful of the labels you give yourself or the ones you allow others to give you because they begin to define your experience. They begin to change what you notice about yourself, what you're willing to try, and what you're not willing to try. This has the potential for far-reaching results and can create a self-fulfilling prophecy. So, guard your heart and mind[8] in terms of what you look at and listen to because there are issues in life that can stem from what is allowed in and "makes itself at home in you." If a person thinks they're "less than," it's unlikely they'll reach for goals they want to achieve, which would further confirm what they've already established in their own minds.

Who you believe you are will ultimately show itself in your actions. When you finally say, "I don't see myself that way anymore," you begin to define who you are and what you will or will not do.

It's harder to change who you are than it is to change your behavior.

What I've learned over the years is that identity is the most important segment in human beings. Who you believe you are or aren't is a major category that can affect the direction of your life. When you know who you are, it's your compass. That becomes your navigational tool. It provides you with what you need to get to where you must go.

Identity

Our identity is our overall collection of things (experiences, relationships, values, memories, and feelings) that define who we are. It's in our identity that we find a crucial component of understanding who we are. Our identity is the strongest force in the human personality. Who do you believe you are, and who do you believe you're not? We need to update it from time to time with a new story to define who we are. When we're able to truly understand who we are, then we can begin to operate in a way that's consistent with that. To put it simply, we can work *with* ourselves rather than *against* ourselves. When we take the necessary time to get to know ourselves, to understand our patterns and what makes us tick, then we begin to tackle how we relate to the rest of the world.

Most of our identity comes from our past experiences, which have shaped who we are. Our journey has left imprints not just on our memories but on our values and our character.

There I was, as a kid in the 1970s, with my mother introducing me to thoughts that affected my life. She would tell me about *The Power of Positive Thinking* and then later had me read the book. This was a self-help book by the American minister Norman Vincent Peale. It provided case histories of how positive thinking helped people achieve a more permanent, optimistic attitude. It talked about positive affirmations and visualizing yourself achieving your dreams. This is the seed that was planted in me at a very early age that took root and began to produce fruit over time. Little did I know at the time that it was expanding my identity.

You can do more in life when you expand your identity.

Your identity can be a heaven or a prison.

We develop our identity most often by what we do. This can be damaging if we build our identity on the building blocks of what we do rather than who we are.

Our relationships are controlled by our identity; people get married and start families based on this. Marriages (and even families) run the risk of being built off false identities or identities based on non-sustaining things.

We need to expand our identity. To do this, we need to face our fears and our perceived limitations. We need to get out of our comfort zones, which can feel like a shock treatment.

The Mask

We have the capacity to put on the mask and compartmentalize our pain. We do this to keep it at bay so that it doesn't become more than we can bear. Though that strategy may work for a period, the pain must eventually be confronted and properly dealt with or else it has the potential to sabotage our future. The mask is a disguise to hide the true identity of something. At some point we must all come face to face with who we are. When all we can see is our pain, we can't truly see who we are and what we can become. It has the potential to impair our vision and thereby stall or even halt our movement.

The Story We Tell Ourselves

The stories we reinforce about ourselves in our minds have the potential to become the backdrop of our real-life story. Whether we realize it or not, we have the power to change our stories and create a different reality for ourselves. This was especially true in my case. As I mentioned earlier, the aftermath of my "day of infamy" moment brought feelings of shame, hurt, and overall feeling like a victim. Even though these feelings that were lodged so deeply inside of me were virtually unseen to my friends, family, and acquaintances, they left an indelible impression on how I saw myself. I knew I had great qualities and a lot of potential, but often I would question whether it was really possible for me to be the person I had dreamed of being before that unforgettable day happened. But let me tell you what I did to slowly dismantle this false narrative that had been erected in my life. This is not an exhaustive list, but it does give the highlights:

1. **Have grace with myself about this story I created in my mind.** I had to be aware of the place I found myself at that point. I also had to acknowledge the truth of my story, but that truth brought so much pain! I did all I could do to avoid it, until I just couldn't anymore. Then I had to take action to change the story I was telling myself. I told myself that was not my condition, it was my conditioning. Though it felt like it was tearing me down, it was building me up and making me strong. It was the conditioning that I needed to continue my journey. At the end of the day, though these things happened to me and it felt so unfair and I felt like I had no control over it, I had to acknowledge that the story was not who I was. I had to take control of how I was interpreting my experience and what I allowed myself to believe about it. I had to forgive myself for thinking that and resolve in my mind not to continually look in the rearview mirror. I had to look ahead to the possibilities of what my life could look like and replace old beliefs and self-talk with new beliefs and self-talk. Finally, I began to appreciate all the lessons that I would ultimately learn along the way.

2. **Detach myself from false truths.** I had to "do my work" of willingly and courageously moving forward despite my extreme discomfort and fear. I had to challenge self-defeating beliefs and negative thoughts that were holding me back from changing my internal story. The more I started challenging these old beliefs, the more I found I had to replace them with more empowering and uplifting ones. This relates to the advice to recite those positive thoughts and statements out loud so you can hear them. No one else may have ever told you these things, and even worse, some may have said the total opposite, but you can become one of the first people to encourage yourself[9].

3. **Start applying more of my strengths to my story.** I had to not only recognize but utilize the unique talents, skills, values, and passions that made me who I was. I had to focus on what I *could* do, rather than what I couldn't. We all have weaknesses—no one is perfect—but it was time for me to focus on my strengths. I also had to use my strengths to overcome my challenges.

4. **Rescript my story.** This is where I stripped away the false narratives that were residing inside of me. I started to rewrite my story from a place of strength and victory rather than from a place of weakness and victimhood, fear, and doubt. I also created a new narrative that accurately reflected my true potential and purpose while aligning with my core values.

5. **I started living as the person I wanted to be.** This involved me aligning my actions with my new story—not just the story I was telling myself, but what I was finally believing. I started practicing new habits that would reinforce this

newfound identity, and I would learn how to celebrate even the smallest progress or achievements.

Position

Definition: "a place where someone or something is located or has been put."

A place. Have you ever looked up and found yourself in "a place"? Sometimes it's a place where you never thought you'd be, or there may have been times when you've found yourself in a place you always hoped to be but never thought it was possible. In either case, the same questions may come to mind: Where am I? And how did I get here?

Where are you positioned? One of the most important things to do is to determine where you are currently positioned in life, and then have the courage to ask yourself where you need to be. This is one of the first steps to navigate your way to your destination.

Believe in Yourself and Who You Were Made to Be

We each have gifts inside of us. It's our job to search and find what those gifts are. Once we do that, we must cultivate the gifts and abilities we have, then create and sustain healthy habits that align with those gifts and abilities. We must not sit on them or take them for granted but instead use those gifts to benefit the world around us. Just think about it: you could be the answer to someone's prayer!

Don't Try to Be Someone Else; Become a Better Version of Yourself

This, I believe, is one of the biggest time and energy wasters that exists: when you try to emulate someone else rather than focusing on developing and expanding your own skills and abilities. By doing that, you can get caught up and can get off-track of your own goals and dreams. You can delay your own development and attainment of goals by over-focusing on what others are doing. Instead, let the accomplishments of others serve as motivation to where you want to be one day, or notice something that they're doing well that you would like to emulate. Go into the lab and learn your strengths, weaknesses, and areas where you need to grow. Be honest with yourself! Know what you do well, and begin to work on yourself.

When you're on the road to being a better version of yourself, it's important to know who you are and what you bring to the table. See yourself in your best-scenario version. See yourself accomplishing that goal, getting that promotion, owning that business, or winning that competition. Tell yourself you can do it! Start your day by being thankful for waking up and having another opportunity to be your better self.

CONSIDER and ASK YOURSELF:

- You are a masterpiece. A one in a 108 billion work of art. Your identity is something that must be recognized for it to grow, and it can affect your behavior.

    » How do you see yourself? How has your identity affected your behavior?

    » If you were asked the question "Who are you?" how would you answer it without using job titles or general demographics like your age or marital status?

- Regardless of the circumstances that brought you into being, you were born. That was not an accident. You were meant to be here, and you have something to offer the world that you can uniquely bring. When you know your worth, you don't settle for less.

- » What step will you take today to remind yourself that you are special and that you're worthy of love?
- » How does your self-image drive your behavior?

- We have the power to change our stories and create a different reality for ourselves. Even in the face of knowing we have great qualities and a lot of potential, we sometimes question whether something is really possible or if we can be the person we dream of being.

  - » What story have you told yourself that you hold onto? Is it working for you or against you?

Chapter 3: Your Relationships

Relationship (*n*): "the way in which two or more concepts, objects, or people are connected, or the state of being connected" (Merriam-Webster)

> **"A good relationship is when someone accepts your past, supports your present, and encourages your future." — Author Unknown**

Who and what we're connected to impacts the extent of our potential and our sustainability. This is a truth that has enormous and life-altering implications. I have found this to be true in my own life.

Over the years, unfortunately by trial and error, I have learned how to navigate my relationships and develop a system of determining who should take part in my life and to what extent they should have access. There's a famous quote that says, "Show me your friends and I'll show you your future." This quote underscores the opening sentence of this chapter. The people, places, and things that we're in relationship with and are connected to will play a significant role in the direction and the destination that will determine our future. Because of this, it's important that we be as sober and intentional about this as we are about where and how we guard our most valuable assets.

In his book *Relational Intelligence: The People Skills You Need for the Life of Purpose You Want*, Dr. Dharius Daniels examines one's ability to define, assign, and manage relationships. He starts by saying: "If you're serious about success and passionate about purpose, you must be intentional about putting the people in your lives—the ones currently there and the ones to come—in the right places." He then defines relational intelligence as "the ability to discern if someone should be a part of our lives and what place they should occupy, and then align them accordingly. It's the ability to appropriately define and align our relationships[10]."

Here is some food for thought. *Who and what you're connected to has the power to propel you or stall you.* It has the capacity to produce power or paralysis. So choose wisely.

Western Michigan University Football Experience

When I think about some of my most impactful relationships, I notice some similar patterns. Notable characteristics include the bond, trust, and respect that formed as we were striving to accomplish a major goal together. In the fall of 1987, I was a freshman free safety on the Western Michigan University football team. We had just hired a new coach who had achieved success at his prior school and was looking to build on that success with this new group of players. That first year, we ended the season with a 5–6 win–loss overall record and were 4–4 in conference play. Looking from the outside, you could say the season was average at best. But behind the scenes was a different story. The making of something great was happening right before our eyes. Even though the final win–loss record didn't reflect it, we were seeing signs of something special happening. Our team won the last two games of the 1987 season in convincing fashion. This, coupled with the return of many of our starting players, gave us a reason to anticipate the 1988 season—so much so that during the offseason, when we were participating in our team winter workout sessions in the old Oakland gym, there was an air of anticipation and excitement for what we knew we could achieve in the upcoming season. We would start and end each workout session with two words shouted in unison—MAC Champs! MAC stood for Mid-American Conference. During the entire offseason, we committed ourselves to that one goal. Every sprint we ran, every weight we lifted, every drill we performed was executed with the precision of a man on a mission.

Fast-forward to the fall camp of 1988. We were going through the tedious "grind it out" process of two-a-days. During one of our player meeting sessions, we asked that all the coaches be excused as we wanted to have a players-only meeting. During that meeting, something special happened that I hadn't experienced prior to that time or even since that time. One by one, guys stood up and started talking about how much of a privilege it was to be a part of this special team and what they were going to commit to doing to make sure that they did their part to help make our shared goal a reality. About midway through that session, guys then started sharing more intimate details about their backgrounds, where they came from, and what they had to overcome just to get to this point. Some of them talked about challenging home-life situations they were going through, while others talked about how the relationships they formed by being a part of this team had made them a better person. Here we were, a group of guys from different geographical, ethnic, and socio-economic backgrounds, all coming together for one common purpose. We talked about how we had each other's backs—no matter what. We talked about how we would manage conflict. We would take it head-on, not run away from it but address it with that person, work it out, and move on, not allowing anything to fester and get in the way of our goal of winning a MAC Championship. We gave each other permission to "check us" if we needed to be checked or corrected at any time. Before that meeting was over, there were some tears, and there were a lot of "I love you, brother"s. We all felt full that day, knowing that we were part of something bigger than ourselves, and because of that, we each felt a sense of obligation and responsibility to do everything we could, individually, to make the team as strong as possible. The upperclassmen were the leaders and led by example, making sure that the younger guys were pulling their share of the weight. There was a shared vision, ownership amongst everyone, open and honest communication, trust, accountability, and genuine love and care for the man next to you. That was the glue that held us together.

To this day, we can all look at that championship ring we earned and be reminded of not only what we accomplished on the football field but the golden nuggets we received that will carry us for the rest of our lives. I got to see, up close, how a championship team is formed and the components that it possesses. We finished the 1988 regular season with nine wins—the most wins our school had ever had in a single season up to that point. We won our first outright conference title and got invited to play in a postseason bowl game. We laid a winning foundation for future Bronco football teams throughout the decades to follow—but it all started from a relationship.

Why Relationships Matter

After the onset of the COVID pandemic, this technological age that we live in has made it easier to go it alone and not invest in relationships. But interpersonal relationships really do matter. Research has found that interpersonal relationships can have several important benefits for both physical and psychological health. These include:

- Combating loneliness
- Increasing resilience to stress
- Decreasing the risk of depression and suicide
- Lowering the risk of cardiovascular disease
- Improving longevity[11]

When you have strong interpersonal relationships, you may feel more motivated to engage in behaviors that are good for your health. Research has also found that people who participate more in social relationships are more likely to eat a healthy diet, exercise regularly, and avoid smoking[12].

While it can be easy to get caught up in the busyness of everyday life, it does us well to make it a habit to spend time cultivating and protecting our relationships with the people who matter the most. The time, attention, and effort we give to others will go a long way in ensuring that we get the same support in return.

Our well-being, be it physical, social, or emotional, in a large part depends on the bonds we form with others as we journey through life. We have the capacity to handle life's challenges better when we have a supportive community of people surrounding us. Because of this, it is important to keep up our relationship skills. While some relationships may not be healthy or helpful and we may have to let them go, other relationships are valuable and worth preserving because they can be a source of comfort and strength when we need them most.

Blind Spots

Establishing, cultivating, and maintaining relationships are also very important because relationship gives people access to us, which in turn enables them to see things in us that we may not be able to see. Simply put, these are our "blind spots." Everyone needs people in their lives who can both identify and then have the courage to speak truth (in love) about things that we can't see. Let this also be a plug to get genuine people in your life who have the capacity and capability to do this. This is especially important if we're trying to get to places where we've never been before. People like this become a critical component to our overall growth and development as we navigate our life's journey to continuously become better versions of ourselves.

At the end of the day, our establishment of and engagement with our relationships is what differentiates us from other creatures on the planet Earth. Each relationship contains a piece of our lives, and because of that, it has the potential to be special. These types of ongoing relationships that we form throughout our lifetimes are what help keep us sane, healthy, and motivated to continuously strive for a better future. It is important that we do our best to maintain these types of relationships for our own best interest as well as the interest of those we love and care about.

Understanding Relationships and the Impacts to Our Development

Who and what we're connected to in life influences what direction we move and what purpose we pursue.

The connections we build with others are critical to our social, emotional, and physical health. Knowing how to maintain interpersonal relationships can help you build the support system that provides strength as you cope with life's challenges. That is why the word "maintaining" is so important in this description. While there are relationships that are worthy of eliminating or letting go, there are other relationships that are worth keeping alive because you will never know when you will need to lean on them. This is where establishing a community comes into play.

One example of this power of community came during a two-month stretch where my mother was in the hospital. Being in her nineties, she was certainly blessed to have lived that long, but she had some health issues that required that she be admitted to the hospital. While she was there, a series of issues arose that progressively spiraled downward. Needless to say, this was very stressful for me and my family as we took trips back and forth to Michigan, and did our due diligence to stay on top of her latest medical updates as they were happening in real time. It was during this time that those relationships that I had developed prior to this were starting to make their true presence known. In this busy and stressful time, I began to lean on the support that these relationships provided to take some of the pressure off. Support came from many different places and in many different forms. The encouragement, prayers, resources (both financial and informational) that me and my family received from my community was truly overwhelming. Even though it was not my intent to establish these relationships for this reason, the benefits they yielded not just to me but to my family were truly amazing and were definitely worth the effort that went into them.

Here are the four most common types of relationships we must learn to navigate well to help us in our overall development as individuals:

1. **Family.** The most important relationship is family. Whether we are born into a family that provided that stable and safe environment for us or one that did just the opposite, our blueprint for effective relationships is greatly influenced by the family environment in which we were raised. Our initial connections are established and nurtured here. This is where we also learn how to deal with conflict, compromise, and our emotional response to those things.

   For example, good family memories can influence your thoughts and direction on having a family or how you will raise children. Similarly, a bad childhood experience or traumatic can even do the same. If left unaddressed, it can drive you in ways that are subtle but have a direct impact on how you handle your family relationships.

2. **Friends.** This relationship has the capacity to provide us with a greater sense of connection and support than the one

that we may experience in our own family. The difference here is that we choose our friends. We don't choose our family; they are naturally given to us. Many times, our friends are the most reliable of the four relationship types. Some of the main components we find in this type of relationship are trust, transparency, unconditional support, common values and interest, and reciprocity.

For example, supportive friendships act as emotional anchors during turbulent times, offering a listening ear and empathy. They can also provide a sounding board for long-term and career decisions and offer encouragement during setbacks. However, we sometimes have people in our lives simply for the sake of not being alone. Others remain in our lives because they've "been a friend for so long" that it just seems like they should be a lifetime friend. In these situations, we may come to realize that these are people who are not propelling parts of our life, or perhaps not even moving in the same direction as we are.

3. **Romantic/Marriage Partners.** These types of relationships are generally the most intimate ones, both emotionally and physically. A healthy relationship with a romantic partner is based on deep bonding, passion, trust, respect, and admiration. As a romantic partner often turns out to be the significant other we share the rest of our lives with, this among all the types of interpersonal relationships is crucial to our survival.

For example, many of us prefer to be in a relationship to share emotional and physical intimacy, but we must be careful not to do it at the risk of our long-term well-being.

Healthy relationships are beneficial and add to our lives in many ways. However, it's important not to lose sight of the goals you are pursuing and how this person fits into them and supports you—not just how they fit into your "today" but if they have the capacity to fit into your "tomorrow." That becomes just as important as who they are.

4. **Work Colleagues.** Strong interpersonal relationships that occur in the workplace benefit the individuals and the company. When employees feel a sense of connection with each other, then a culture of healthy work habits can form, which can also increase productivity and results.

   For example, having strong interpersonal relationships at work creates a sense of belonging. The frequent interactions, commonalities, and mutual interests can sometimes develop into authentic friendships. However, it's important to understand that even acquaintances that have those characteristics still may not be friends. Some acquaintances engage in office gossip with other co-workers. It is important to avoid participating in this as it could lead to a negative work environment and potentially harm your reputation. To keep healthy workplace relationships, enjoy the connections while being polite, but be wise at the same time.

How we manage all these relationships is vitally important to our overall success, plays a significant role in how we feel about ourselves, and affects the lens through which we view the world. *Effectively navigating our relationships, just like our distinction, provides us the awareness we need to determine where we currently stand, and then helps us to determine where we're going.*

SPIRITUAL MARKER: The four most common relationships—those that involve our family, our friends, our romantic/marriage partners, and our work colleagues—are horizontal in nature. But there is one more relationship that I've found to be essential for my overall quality of life, and that is my vertical relationship with God. When this vertical relationship is prioritized and cultivated, it adds much-needed perspective to my horizontal relationships.

Relationships Can Either Stall Us or Propel Us

I talked a little earlier about how relational intelligence is an important piece of our overall development. On our journey in life, we should get "under the hood" and perform a diagnostic on our relationships, looking at who we choose to share our time, space, and resources with. Whether it be in a friendship, a marriage, a business venture, or whatever else, it has the potential to affect the speed and direction that we end up traveling in our lives. That relationship may cause us to either stall or pull away from our quest or propel us toward our desired destination. Who we're in relationship with will also influence whether we feel good about the direction we're moving in and will serve as a catalyst to continue moving forward with the pace and persistence of someone on a mission. I call this a directional push. The flip side of this is when that person you're in relationship with has no idea of what your journey entails and has the potential to serve as an inhibitor, either slowing down or even stopping your overall development. So, again, it's important to take the time and be intentional to choose wisely. It is important, with both new and existing relationships, to determine who will influence your time, space, direction, and the pace of your journey. The stakes are too high to leave it to chance. Not only will it affect you, but it will also affect those who look to you for direction, guidance, and resources.

CONSIDER and ASK YOURSELF:

- Who and what we're connected to impacts the extent of our potential and our sustainability. On our journey in life, we should get under the hood and perform a diagnostic on our relationships, looking at whom we choose to share our time, space, and resources with.

  » How would you rate your closest relationships? Are they helping propel you toward your potential or not, on a scale of 1 to 10 (with 10 being the best)?

- Sometimes we have people in our lives for the sake of "not being alone." It could be because they've "been a friend for so long" that it just seems like they should be a lifetime friend.

  » How does the success or failure of your past relationships drive you?

- Everyone needs people in their lives who can both identify and then have the courage to speak truth (in love) about things that we can't see.

  » Who do you have in your life who can speak truth to you and reveal blind spots?

  » If you don't have anyone, what will you do to identify someone who can be such a person to you?

PART 2: Acknowledgment: Where Are You Going?

Acknowledge (*v*): "to accept or admit the existence or truth of something. It can also mean to recognize the fact or importance or quality of something" (Merriam-Webster)

> **"The acknowledgment of a single possibility can change everything." —Aberjhani**

Imagine how awesome it would be if we could just be ourselves and do what we love. If we could listen to our inner voice and follow our heart. If we could act on what matters to us, what excites us, and what makes us feel alive. If we could be brave and honest, without worrying about what others think or say. If we could share our gifts and talents, without holding anything back or settling for less. If we could find our community and grow together. If we could do what makes us happy and helps the world around us.

How do we find what is deep inside of us and then do something with it? This is about scanning, diagnosing, and aligning ourselves in a way that puts us in the best possible position to achieve excellence and success. In Part 1: Awareness, we realized that before doing anything, we must first discover where we are. In Part 2: Acknowledgment, we must determine where we are going. I introduced the need to perform periodic diagnostics on your relationships; now I am going to expound on the use of a car engine diagnosis. Whether your vehicle is showing signs of a problem or not, a full car diagnostic test can help pinpoint if there is a problem. The diagnostic test relies on a computer system that links to the vehicle's processor, sensors, and microchips, logging any problems or issues present. It can reveal any existing flaws, including problems with the exhaust, transmission, oil tank, and other systems. Its value comes into being because of its ability to help pinpoint issues quickly and reliably without the need for a full-scale vehicle inspection[13].

Just as it is important that we have a diagnostic performed on our vehicle, especially if we plan on taking a trip, we should periodically run a check on ourselves, especially as we enter new seasons or transitional periods of our lives. This section is about acknowledgment—accepting or admitting the existence or truth of something, as well as recognizing the fact or importance or quality of that same thing. It will start with examining our ability to accept and admit the existence of our purpose through the thing(s) that we're passionate about. In almost any situation where the acceptance or admittance of a thing is needed to move forward to the next chapter, this becomes a critical piece to conquer, for it will require pushing past obstacles and being honest and transparent with yourself about yourself. *Acknowledgment is not just about the recognition of the existence and truth of something, but the ability to fully embrace it* in order to act on it. While it is noteworthy to recognize that you have a purpose, the goal should ultimately be to pursue it with dedication and passion.

You may be thinking, "I can't do that! That's too challenging, too uncomfortable!" But guess what, *if you wanna get there, you gotta go there!* Yes, sometimes "going there" means confronting your fears, your doubts, and your insecurities—those things you swore you would never revisit again. Though it may require us to change our mindsets, our habits, and behaviors, it can be empowering and liberating, because it has the potential to unlock the chains of stagnation and settling for less than that which we were created for. Let me just state the obvious: this stuff ain't easy! But it's so necessary and so worth it. Not just to you, but those who you have responsibility for or influence over. They will also benefit because of your decision.

Lastly, acknowledgment isn't a one-time thing. It's a continual process. I can't tell you the number of times I have to "check in" with myself to see how I'm coming along to make sure I'm aligning with my purpose. In doing that, I must be open to new opportunities, new feedback, and new insights that will play a major role in my growth. So, with that being said, let's buckle up and get ready as we continue our journey.

Chapter 4:
Your Inspiration

Inspiration (*n*): "the process of being mentally stimulated to do or feel something, especially to do something creative" (Merriam-Webster)

"What lies behind us and lies before us are small matters compared to what lies within us." —Ralph Waldo Emerson

Each of us has a flame inside of us that needs to be found, fostered, and fueled.

It has often been said that the two most important days of your life are the day you were born and the day you realize *why* you were born. Each and every one of us has a reason for being here, and whether we realize it or not, there is a purpose assigned to our existence. Now, whether our purpose comes to pass or not depends largely on us. Yet, the fact remains, there is a purpose for our life. Regardless of the circumstances of how we came into this world, whether they were favorable or unfavorable ones, the fact that we are here and are recorded in time and history is an indication that none of us is a mistake and there is something meaningful we are to do while we are here. Whether we choose to find our purpose in life or not, it is in us and it behooves us to take the journey to figure out what it is. You were created for a purpose, and it's this purpose that can add to our life in ways we can't imagine. It's what gives our life meaning and a sense of direction; it's what helps us make choices in our lives while affecting how we act or respond in certain situations.

I love the Ralph Waldo Emerson quote that says, "What lies behind us and lies before us are small matters compared to what lies within us." No truer words have been spoken. The true prize is lodged within each of us. With that being said, let's examine three things that relate to our inspiration or purpose. They are:

1. Find It (Search and Discover It)

2. Foster It (Protect and Nurture It)

3. Fuel It (Maximize and Share It)

1. Finding Your Purpose

As we journey to discover our purpose, we shouldn't have to travel that far to see the first signs of it. Why, you ask? It's because there will be signs that can help you to find your way. Some signs are:

- It will be something that energizes you and makes you feel motivated while you're doing it.
- You can do it and not feel overwhelmingly taxed.
- It's something you can do with relative ease, and it comes naturally to you.

Chapter 4: Your Inspiration

Deep inside each of us, there is a natural desire that brings a certain amount of passion, joy, and contentment. It's what drives us. As we discussed earlier, knowing and understanding yourself is important for many reasons. However, as it relates to our purpose, it helps us to identify those unique skills and talents that we possess and can use to not only benefit ourselves, but those around us. When I think about this in my own life, it has been writing and helping people through encouragement, instruction, and providing direction to others, whether it was during times of reflection or during times of crisis. This has always been my inspiration. In every season of my life I have encouraged, instructed, and provided direction to people and have always felt a sense of passion, motivation, and contentment from it. One of my earliest examples of this was seeing my mother, who was a longtime, dedicated community advocate and resource person. She would take me with her to everything from board meetings to strategy sessions to being with her in the office while she did her work. I would hear her conversations with those she worked with and could see the looks in people's eyes that she's helped along the way. Whether it be providing specific informational resources to help them in certain situations or giving encouragement to someone who desperately needed it, the looks on their faces expressed reassurance and confidence. At the time, I didn't realize how much I enjoyed those kinds of interactions, and I later realized that I wanted to have that with people.

It's very important that we establish a reason to do what we do. This will help to keep us focused when internal and external forces attempt to stall or halt our progress. Whenever this happens, always revisit the purpose. *Your purpose will be your shield against the onslaught of two of the biggest opponents to purpose: fear and doubt.* As we're traveling along our way, we inevitably arrive at a fork in the road where we ask ourselves, "Am I going to be who I really am, and who my inner self is leaning toward, or am I going to be who others expect me to be?" This question can only be answered by you, and hopefully you take the necessary time and effort to search for and discover the answer.

This assessment tool called "Your Purpose GPS" will help you identify themes throughout your life to help you discover your purpose.

Personal Assessment Tool: Your Purpose GPS

A GPS is a Global Positioning System. It's primarily used to determine where you are on Earth and helps you to get from one place to another. It can be used to help you track or monitor movement or changes in position.

As you reflect on your journey through life, recognize that there has been a story being told in the background. Some things can be clearly and easily detected, in terms of what you like or don't like, while other things are more subtle. You have been taking road trips from one place to another in your journey of life, and a story has been building in the background.

The Purpose GPS is designed to help you track the course that your life's journey has taken. As you complete the following assessment to help uncover elements of your purpose, allow yourself time to reflect and concentrate on the questions asked. You have spent many years of your life to get to where you are today, and you may have many experiences and memories to reflect upon. So consider all of this as you complete this assessment.

For this assessment you will:

1) Review three essential components used to uncover the story that's been told in the background of your life.

2) Read each question and look over the course of your life, which is your storyline, your journey.

3) Provide an answer for two general stages of your life for each question.

Stage 1: Your Childhood and Adolescent Years (10–17 years old)

Stage 2: Your Young Adult and Adult Years (18 years old to today)

Let's start by examining three essential components:

- **Blueprint:** This symbolizes the most impactful lessons, values, or characteristics you received that influenced how you lived.

- **Design:** This symbolizes those things that came *easy for you to do*, and you found it fulfilling. These served as bright moments in your life.

- **Framework:** This symbolizes the essential environments and activities that *energized* you and *nurtured* your growth and maturity.

Write your response for each stage as you reflect on your life from your childhood/adolescent years (Stage 1) into young adult/adulthood (Stage 2).

Part 1—Identify Your Components

Essential Component 1: Blueprint (impactful lessons, values, or characteristics that *influenced* how you lived)

- What impactful lesson was established in the childhood/adolescent stage of your life that influenced how you lived?

For example, one of the most impactful guides in my adolescent stage was a person, my little league football coach, Godfrey Jones, who helped me to understand two critical things: first, that what I possessed inside of me was greater than the challenges that stood in front of me, and second, that when I take care of my primary responsibilities first, I can then enjoy the fruits of my hard work that would follow. I incorporated those principles into my life, and it helped to reinforce the foundation of my work ethic.

Then for Stage 2, identify an impactful lesson that was established in your adulthood, and write your response below.

Stage 1 (Childhood/Adolescence):

Stage 2 (Young Adult/Adulthood):

Essential Component 2: Design (those things that came *easy* for you and were fulfilling)

- What things came easy for you and, as you did them, gave you fulfillment?

For example, as long as I can remember, I have been an encourager and leader of my peers. Whether it was participating with them in either my athletic pursuits or just in everyday life, providing words of motivation and encouragement came easy for me. As I'd work toward my dreams, I would encourage others to work toward theirs. I loved the feeling that I would get from helping to have a positive influence in someone else's life.

Then for Stage 2, identify those things that came easy for you and were fulfilling in your adulthood, and write your response below.

Stage 1 (Childhood/Adolescence):

Stage 2 (Adulthood):

Essential Component 3: Framework (those environments or activities you feel have been *essential* in your life and that *energize* you)

- What environments or activities energize you and are an essential part of your life?

For example, being raised by a single mother in the church, I embraced her teachings of strength, hard work, and diligence. These values, along with a deep sense of God's omnipresence and the significance of faith, formed the foundational core of my being and guided my life choices.

Then for Stage 2, identify those environments or activities that are an essential part of your adulthood, and write your response below.

Stage 1 (Childhood/Adolescence):

Stage 2 (Adulthood):

Part 2—Identify Your Key Descriptors

Now, go back and circle the words and phrases that were impactful to your life in each of the three essential components.

For example, my Stage 1 circled words and phrases from the three essential components would look like this:

Essential Component 1—Stage 1 (Childhood/ Adolescent):
Take care of responsibilities; self-worth

Essential Component 2—Stage 1 (Childhood/Adolescence):
Leader; encourager; positive influencer

Essential Component 3—Stage 1 (Childhood/Adolescence):
Strong; hard work; diligence; God; faith

Now, write the words and phrases you circled from the three essential components that were impactful to your life.

Essential Component 1—Stage 1 (Childhood/Adolescence):

Essential Component 2—Stage 1 (Childhood/Adolescence):

Essential Component 3—Stage 1 (Childhood/Adolescence):

Essential Component 1—Stage 2 (Adulthood):

Essential Component 2—Stage 2 (Adulthood):

Essential Component 3—Stage 2 (Adulthood):

NOTE: There may be words and phrases that overlap as you move into Adulthood (Stage 2).

Part 3—Identify Your Themes

Take a panoramic view of your life and see what common themes or patterns have appeared. There can be variation as you change, grow, and develop in your life. However, you'll also find some things have stayed consistent and stood the test of time.

For example:

Blueprint

Common theme: I tend to like helping others, caring for others.

Design

Common theme: I feel very fulfilled when I am a positive influence and lead others.

Framework

Common theme: I feel those things that are a natural and fundamental part of who I am are being a strong, faith-filled person, who encourages others.

Take a panoramic view of your life looking at both Stage 1 and Stage 2. Write the themes you see emerging.

Blueprint

Common theme:

Design

Common theme:

Framework

Common theme:

Look at what has been building at the core of you and ask yourself these two questions: "What is inside of me that needs to be further explored, developed, and maximized?" and "Am I currently operating in the area that is my purpose, or am I trying to get there?"

This assessment is a guide to identify those things that have shaped you and demonstrate what you are naturally drawn to. That is what you further explore and incorporate into your life and work toward fulfilling as your purpose. Now that you've identified what you're naturally drawn to, let's now see what you must do to foster it—to nurture and protect it.

2. Fostering Your Purpose

Once we've taken the necessary time and effort to find those things that have shaped us and that we are naturally drawn to, we must cultivate the gifts and abilities we have, then create, and sustain healthy habits that align with those gifts and abilities. This will help us keep them protected and nurtured. Imagine being able to wake up each morning with a clear sense of purpose. To do that, we must not sit on gifts and abilities but use them to benefit the world around us. Just think about it: you could be the answer to someone's prayer!

Keeping the "Pilot Light" on for Your Dreams

Sometimes you have to do what you have to do in order to one day do what you want to do. When the time and the situation doesn't allow for you to actively pursue the passion inside of you (your purpose), you have to put those dreams on hold. I call this period keeping the "pilot light" on your dreams, because one day it will be ignited. Don't allow the monotony of the day-to-day routine and struggle snuff out your dreams. Diligently work on yourself and your gifts while you wait! Discipline is of utmost importance during this period. *Discipline is the "force field" that keeps your dreams protected from complacency.*

Now, for those of you reading this who are unfamiliar with a pilot light, this is a small flame, usually in a furnace or stove, that remains burning with a small amount of gas even when the appliance is turned off. This serves as an ignition source when the appliance is turned back on. Growing up in the 1970s in Michigan, I remember seeing the small flame still burning even while the furnace was in a state of dormancy. The fact that it was continuously burning, even ever so slightly, provided a reassuring promise that that fire would blaze when the right conditions presented themselves.

The very fact that I am writing this book is evidence that my pilot light has remained burning for years, whether it was through adverse conditions or favorable but untimely ones.

Here are a few tips for keeping the pilot light on for your dreams as you foster your purpose:

- **Keep the fire going "out of season" so that it's ready for your "in season."**

    Create a plan. Break your goals down into smaller, bite-size steps you can do on a day-to-day (or week-by-week) basis and feel good about it while you're doing it. This becomes your plan to keep the pilot light on your dream.

    Stay focused. This can be extremely difficult, especially with so many things competing for our attention. Don't allow distractions from achieving your goals and realizing your purpose. Designate time to work toward your goal and make it a routine, even if it is once a week. Set the time to make it happen.

    After you've kept that bite-size time, *reward yourself.* Tie a reward to the task to train your brain that upon completion of that time, you deserve a reward. A reward doesn't have to be anything big. Maybe it's a treat of some sort, a small trip to an enjoyable place you don't get to visit often, or just some "chill time" doing your favorite activity.

- **Make the most of your time when you're in your "waiting season."**

  Stay motivated. This is where you remember your "why"—why you even started on this journey. Don't allow yourself to continuously look through the rearview mirror, but keep focused on the goal at hand.

  Create a supportive community. Surround yourself with people who believe in you and support your goals and aspirations and can speak life and encouragement into you. You also want people who can challenge you when necessary. This is essential in your overall growth and development.

- **Allow yourself to go through the process of overall self-discipline, responsibility, and developing healthy habits.**

  Take care of yourself. Make sure you're taking care of yourself mentally, physically, spiritually, and emotionally. This will help keep you on track and not easily derailed.

  Make good choices. Your choices will either keep you on the road to your purpose or on a road leading away from your purpose. Take the time to look over the patterns of your life and see which decisions and activities have served you well and which have not. Be honest enough to acknowledge each, tell yourself the truth about it, and make appropriate changes as needed.

- **Continue to work on your gift during your waiting season, and improve your personal intangibles during this time.**

Exercise leadership. This skill involves taking initiative, motivating others, and making decisions. You can improve your leadership by finding a mentor, taking on new challenges, communicating clearly, and learning from your mistakes.

Be flexible. There are times when we'll have to adjust our plans or timelines due to the unpredictability of life. When this happens, we must adjust and adapt to the new reality while keeping our eyes on the prize.

Nurture the Authentic You

To nurture the authentic you, you must know who you are, or else you'll be feeding something that is not consistent with who you are. Take the time to get to know yourself again. What were some common patterns in your assessment? What inspires you? What pulls at your heart strings? What gets your juices flowing when the subject is brought up?

When you are being authentic, you not only do those things that bring you personal satisfaction, but you do them in a way that is unique and tailored to you—in only the way that you'll do it. You are not trying to be someone else but just being yourself and being totally comfortable in your own skin. There is no one on the planet like you—not one! Given that, you don't have to spend time and resources trying to be someone else or travel in their lane. *Create your own lane, and travel it often!*

SPIRITUAL MARKER: I've learned that God didn't make any mistakes when he created us. Every little idiosyncrasy and characteristic that each of us has is totally a part of us. Strive to become a better version of yourself every day! In doing so, you will become better than you were previously. Don't try to be someone else. It's a waste of your time, and you won't be good at it anyway! Spend time tending to your own garden, watering and nurturing it (through the sun and the rain), and watch it turn into a thing of beauty. Embrace who you are! As I mentioned earlier, you are an original. There never has been, nor will there ever be another like you. You are more than enough. Know that it's not an overnight process, but it is a process that, if stuck to, will yield unbelievable results because you invested in yourself.

Your dreams are like jewels. They not only have intrinsic value, but they have the potential to have value far exceeding our own expectations. We must protect and nourish our dreams and give them "real-world" opportunities to reveal themselves.

Some things in life are like weeds, and they come to snuff out the live plants that are growing in your garden. These weeds are things like past hurts, pains, damaging relationships, and even your own pride. Discipline serves to keep you on track to have that awareness and acknowledgment so that you can put new practices in place to achieve your goals.

Never forget your *why*. Your *why* is where your motivation lies. No one reaches their dreams without motivation. What better motivation is there than to know your *why*? Your *why* must be visited often to remind you of where you've been to propel you to where you're going!

Sometimes we get so focused on the *what* and we often lose sight of the *why*. What's in the *why*? It's your reason for not giving up, even when you want to.

Establish your *why*, and keep it in front of you!

When you lose your why, you lose your way. Always remember your why because it must be compelling enough for you to keep going, even when you want to give up. On February 11, 1990, Buster Douglas achieved the impossible in many people's eyes. He defeated the undefeated, undisputed heavyweight champion of the world, Mike Tyson. Anyone who can remember Mike Tyson in his prime knows that this is widely considered as the greatest upset in professional sports history. The oddsmakers gave Douglas a 1 in 50 chance of winning the fight. So even from an oddsmaker's point of view, they saw it was possible for Douglas to win, but extremely improbable. You see, Buster Douglas's mother had died just prior to the fight. Though Tyson knocked him down during the fight, his mother's death and what she meant to him motivated him to get back up off that canvas floor and continue fighting ferociously to ultimately win the fight and take over the title belt to become the new heavyweight champion of the world. The point here is that no matter how improbable something may be, there's always a possibility that it can actually happen. What makes something so highly improbable possible? The *why*! Your *why* is strong enough to control your will (or your reason) and help you to make your way. You see, Buster's purpose during this fight was to honor his mother's memory in the only way possible, and that was to do whatever it took to win, no matter the obstacle. It was the strength of his *why* that made an improbable event possible. *The strength of your why will make what seems improbable possible.*

Your *why* is your reason, and your reason is powerful. The more compelling your reason becomes, the more significant is the role your *why* plays. Your reason is what makes you get up when you are down. It will help you continue moving forward when you feel like you can't go any further. Your *why* is your guidepost and what moves you in the right direction.

Your gift can open the way for good things to happen in your life and bring you into the presence of great people[14]. Cultivate the gift inside of you. You have great things inside of you that are literally waiting to "catch some air."

3. Fueling Your Purpose

After we've identified the essential components that lead us toward discovering our purpose and then foster them until we can fully pursue it, we then want to fuel our purpose. This is the ultimate aim once we find our purpose. In practical terms, fuel is a substance that is burned to produce heat or power. We want to fuel our purpose so that it can produce power to achieve all it was meant to achieve and become all it was meant to become—to maximize and share it.

SPIRITUAL MARKER: I've learned in my own life that there are some things that I won't always have 100 percent certainty about. Things will happen that will shake or threaten what you have believed to be true. But faith is what we possess on the inside that is later manifested in our actions. Romans 10:17 says, "So then faith cometh by hearing, and hearing by the word of God." Faith is only as good as the "feet" that we attach to it. In other words, faith isn't faith unless it's displayed in our attitude, our actions, and who we align ourselves with. James 2:26 says, "For as the body without the spirit is dead, so faith without works is dead also." So continuing to walk (and not freeze) is important.

Fear[15], on the other hand, is defined as an unpleasant and often strong emotion caused by anticipation or awareness of danger. Our bodies do not know the difference between thoughts that are from real and present danger or ones that are assumed. This is where the acronym "False Evidence Appearing Real (FEAR)" comes from. Many of our fears are learned and originate from our thoughts. Our negative emotions are triggered, and our bodies respond[16]. Faith can inspire us to overcome challenges and pursue our dreams with passion, while fear can limit us, hold us back, and render us ineffective.

Weighing the Cost of Your Fears

There are two fears that I had to wrestle with: The Fear of Doing It (and Failing), and The Fear of Not Doing It (and Regret). What I've learned is that there are costs associated with each of these fears. The question then became, "Can I live with the costs?" I had to remind myself of the benefits associated with doing it and not just the costs. Too many times we give the cost factor all the weight, but we don't give the benefit factor the amount of weight it deserves. Rather than focusing on what happens if it doesn't work, start playing in your head, "But what if it does work?" and then take small baby steps toward it. Once you find yourself taking steps in that direction, no matter how small they may be, start playing this scenario in your head: "What am I going to do *when* it works?" What you've essentially done is taken your mind and your intentions from an *if* mindset to a *when* mindset. You then continue to make steps, no matter how small, in this direction with a *when* mindset that does not possess an "out" clause. You're not giving yourself an out. You're basically saying, "It's going to happen! I'm committing myself to giving everything I've got to make this endeavor become a reality."

In this game of life, we must play to win! Don't play to not lose! For anyone who watches a football game, either live or on TV, you've seen a game where a team has the lead with a few minutes left to play in the game and then suddenly they go conservative on us, running three simple handoff plays and getting minimal yardage, even on third down. Rather than running plays that will have a higher likelihood of getting a first down, they choose to play it safe, go three and out, and punt the ball to the opposing team, only to watch that team aggressively put their two-minute drive together and win the game in the waning seconds. Why did the winning team win? Because they played to win and didn't play it safe with an attempt to "back" themselves into a win rather than "drive" to a win. You have to press toward your win, your purpose, your prize.

Dismantling Fear and Exercising Faith

One of the biggest obstacles we may face is the seemingly insurmountable mountain called "our past." Why does this seem like it's insurmountable? The pain of our past tends to make us block it out to avoid looking at it, so we never get a chance to see it for what it truly is. Sometimes it's something that happened to us, in us, or around us that did not have a favorable outcome and left us in a bad state, either mentally, physically, emotionally, or spiritually.

Your mind and brain are ready to process fear to keep you alert and safe. We need that to help us avoid doing something that may cause danger, be a threat, or put us in harm's way. That is healthy fear. Another type of fear comes from pain and can cause you to want to run from certain memories of the past. You may rationalize why you shouldn't bring these memories up and convince yourself to "leave the past in the past" to move on, though you know there is still pain or anger there, creating tender spots in your emotions. It can make you feel vulnerable to admit or discuss these topics. You may feel weak from guilt, shame, or regret. That fear keeps you from wanting to address these tender spots and holds you back from freedom, potential emotional and mental healing, and so much more. To dismantle it allows you to break it down so you can build on new, healthy habits to realize your inspiration.

Here are three strategies to dismantle your fears:

1. Change how you view yourself and your fears.

    - You have more power than you know. Fear will make you feel helpless and weak. You have an opportunity to take control of your life and your fears.

    - When all you can see is your pain, then you can't see what is over the horizon for you. *Your negative experiences are to be learned from, not to be lived in.*

    - When addressing your negative past experiences, you may find it difficult and uncomfortable to go down certain roads that challenge you. Some of these roads are not meant for you to walk alone. Seeking a support group or a professional mental health provider is key[17]. My family and I have greatly benefited from our family therapist for some years now. We knew we had challenges that we just weren't equipped to take on by ourselves, and by having an objective third person, skilled in that area, to help us was life changing for us. We rose from many challenges healthy, confident, and hopeful each time.

2. Don't run away from the roar—run *to* it!

- Let's look at fear as a response to a lion's roar. A lion's roar can be heard from as far as five miles away. A lion's roar can also paralyze you. Elizabeth von Muggenthaler, a bio acoustician from the Fauna Communications Research Institute in North Carolina, discovered that when a lion gives a deep, loud roar, its prey could experience paralysis on the spot[18]. So it's understandable how a lion's deep, loud roar could have a paralyzing effect on its prey.

- Many times, your reward is in the mouth of the roaring lion. That sounds scary, right? Well, every roar is not from a lion, though it could seem like it. Your natural tendency may be to run *away* from the roar, but to run away from the roar can sometimes run you into the grips of a pack of real lions waiting for you. Fear can seem like a lion and move you in a direction that you were never intended to go. However, when your energy and focus aim toward the achievement of something—rather than the losing or non-achievement of it—you stand a greater likelihood of achieving it than if you focused on the fear itself.

- *Don't run away from your pain, run toward it. Make a decision to conquer it! Somewhere in your pain, your purpose will reveal itself.* You have an opportunity to not let your fear hijack your dreams. Run toward that roaring fear.

- Running toward the roar addresses fear and how to not only overcome it but use it to catapult you into your destiny. Anything worth having is worth fighting for. We are built to be strong and courageous[19], but sometimes circumstances can intimidate us, and we choose not to move forward. You have what it takes to work toward your purpose and dreams. *When your passion and desire become greater than your fears, success is not just possible, it's inevitable.*

3. Focus on your dream, gifts, and skills daily to help propel you forward.

    - Don't focus on the mountain in front of you, but focus on the desired outcome and the path for you to get over that mountain.
    - Speak to your mountain, refocus your thoughts on your dream daily, and have faith that you can move it.
        » The next section, which focuses on action, will get you moving, but you have to start with your thoughts.
    - In her book *Switch On Your Brain*, Dr. Caroline Leaf speaks on neuroplasticity, which speaks to how your brain can be rewired.
        » She states that you must choose to control your thought life.
        » This helps to rewire a positive thought network and destroy old negative ones[20].
    - The mountain may be big, but you have the power to change how you see it and the thoughts that come behind it.

> » Fear seeks to drive you away from your purpose, show you every mountain with past pain and hurts, and entice you to be comfortable in a state outside of your purpose.
>
> » Imagine this: the past hurt that was meant to hold you back or destroy the faith you need to progress can propel you into your purpose once you run to it and address it.

SPIRITUAL MARKER: God wants to grow you. Whenever he's growing you, it will feel very uncomfortable. True growth is never comfortable—and it will always require dependence on walking with God, not operating independent of him. I've found that just as there is a God who loves me and wants my success, there is an enemy who wants to work against my happiness, success, and life. The enemy's plan is to get us off track from what God has planned for us. We have a purpose, and the enemy has a strategy of fear to keep us from it. Therefore, to operate in fear is counterintuitive to our success.

Beware

There was a time when I used success and achievement to attempt to drown out the pain. That worked for quite a while, but eventually I had to come face-to-face with the pain and deal with it. What had put my achievement into overdrive was that I needed a distraction and compartmentalized my pain. I needed a way to block out the pain and anesthetize it.

It isn't until we dare to visit the dark alleys of our pain, and the process that goes with it, that we can come to find our true purpose. When we finally have an awareness and an acceptance of what has happened, then we can take the necessary course of action to address it.

Use Faith to Fuel Your Vehicle and Overcome Your Fears

The moment you don't live in fear is the moment you will be free. Fear seeks to flatten your tires and immobilize you and render you stranded in a place you were never intended to be. Faith fuels and mobilizes. Let faith fuel your journey to your purpose, your potential, and ultimately your destiny. Faith sets you on a course designed to get you to your intended destination, reserved just for you.

You maximize your purpose when you allow it to become a benefit not just to you but to others as well. This happens when you intentionally create opportunities to make your gifts, talents, and abilities both known and available to others.

Don't forget Ralph Waldo Emerson's quote at the beginning of this chapter: "What lies behind us and lies before us are small matters compared to what lies within us." Each of us has a flame inside of us that needs to be found, fostered, and fueled. When we've taken the time and energy it takes to do that, we give ourselves an opportunity to be all we can be and do all there is for us to do.

CONSIDER and ASK YOURSELF:

What's the fuel that's driving you? In what direction has it taken you? To a place of contentment or discontent? The direction of your life ultimately determines your destination.

- **FIND IT:** Many people have wondered why they were born or why they exist in this world. It behooves us to search for and find it. Once you find it, that becomes your *why*. It's important to share it with others as it can benefit both you and them.

  » What have you done to determine the purpose for which you were born and why you exist in the world?
    » Are you willing (and will you) look at your skills and abilities and those natural desires that bring a certain amount of passion, joy, and contentment to discover your purpose?
  » What is your *why*, and how will it benefit others around you?

- **FOSTER IT**: Sometimes you have to do what you have to do in order to one day do what you want to do.

  » What plan(s) have you established to take small daily or weekly steps to keep the pilot light on for your dream?
    » If you haven't taken small steps, take time now to outline specific steps with a time frame for completion.
  » What community (it can be two or more people) have you connected with who believes in you and supports your dream with encouragement?
    » If you don't have one, it's important to find one!

- **THE AUTHENTIC YOU**: This is not only doing what brings you personal satisfaction but doing it in a way that is unique and tailored to you—in the way that only you will do it.

> » Have you taken time to get to know yourself and discover what inspires you or gets your juices flowing when the subject is brought up?
>> » If you haven't, reflect on the Purpose GPS and see what you are naturally drawn to.

- **FUEL IT**: We want to fuel our purpose to produce power to help us achieve and become all we were meant to be. Uncovering what fuels you and in what direction it's taking you is key.

> » What is the fuel that drives you? Is it faith or fear?
> » If fear has driven you, are you ready (and willing) to take steps to dismantle fear and exercise faith to build your faith stronger each day?
>> » Outline how you would do this and in what time frame you would do it.

PART 3: Action: How Are You Going to Get There?

Action (*n*): "the fact or process of doing something, typically to achieve an aim" (Merriam-Webster)

> "Those who don't jump will never fly."
> —Leena Ahmad Almashat

We have talked about awareness, both from an internal self-awareness standpoint (that focuses on those things we know, think, and feel about ourselves) and an external self-awareness standpoint (that focuses on how others perceive you). We have also talked about acknowledgment, examining how the admittance of a thing is needed to move forward to the next chapter. Finally, we're going take the next step along the journey in which taking *action* is the goal. Though obstacles and detours will distract you from your desired results, don't let that be your primary focus. Also, we must remember what not taking action has the potential to do. Even if we've experienced failure in the past, we should not allow that to define who we are or whether we take action in the future. We should look at our failures through a lens of lessons learned. Because if we do that, then we can become willing to learn even more. Taking action allows us to stretch ourselves beyond what we can see while setting the building blocks of trust within ourselves and, at the same time, seizing the opportunities of the present. To break free from the average, you need to shift into the gear of taking action. This is how we continue to make progress toward our goals while we're on our journey. **Your journey's success isn't just tied to outcomes or results but to the growth and development that you experience along the way.**

This is the stage where you take what you know, and you move on. It's like the adage from the late American poet Maya Angelou, "When you know better, you do better." It means that we should always strive to do the best we can with the knowledge and skills we have, and when we learn more or improve ourselves, we should act accordingly. It is a quote that inspires us to embrace change and growth in our lives.

Chapter 5:
Your Vision

Vision (*n*): "the act or power of seeing: sight"; "a thought, concept, or object formed by the imagination"; "a manifestation to the senses of something immaterial" (Merriam-Webster)

> **"Having a vision for your life allows you to live out of hope, rather than out of your fears." —Steadman Graham**

You have taken the time to create an awareness of yourself as well as your surroundings, and you have examined who and what you're connected to in the form of relationships and how they either serve or don't serve you. You've then acknowledged and recognized your passion that leads to your purpose, and now there is a resounding call to action by having a vision to see your life not just as it stands today but what it has the potential to become. When you apply vision to your future, you can create a mental picture that can be used to direct your action. *Vision* serves as a guide and can be used to project your purpose. It also *serves as the road through which your goals and aspirations travel.* These goals and aspirations can keep you motivated, make you accountable, help you stay on track, give you a way to measure your progress, and provide a sense of accomplishment. In every facet of life, having a vision is very important. Whatever obstacles or roadblocks you may face, when you have a clear vision of what you want to happen, you can make better decisions. In this section I outline the benefits of having a vision and how to create and pursue your vision.

There are two things a vision can help you produce:

1) A plan that points you in the direction you want to go

2) A disciplined commitment to the plan to take you to the destination

Vision doesn't nullify your plans; vision inspires them! When you have a vision, it will inspire you to create a plan that will attempt to bring it to fruition.

Your commitment to your vision is only as strong as the disciplined habits that you establish to reach it. Without disciplined habits to keep you aligned with attaining your vision, you may have to revisit your commitment to whether you really want this or not.

When you want something badly enough, you'll figure out a way to get it. Why? Because dreams produce motivation, and motivation produces the creativity, ingenuity, and discipline required to stay the course, despite the obstacles that will come.

Remember, a vision is only as effective as the commitment tied to it.

The Benefits of Having Vision

Do you have a vision for your life? A vision is not just a fancy word for a wish or a dream. It is a powerful tool that can help you design your future and live your best life. *A vision is a clear and compelling picture of what you want to achieve in the future and how you want to live your life.* It's based on your values, passions, and strengths, and it reflects your true and authentic self.

There are four benefits that having a vision for your life brings:

- **Clarity:** A vision helps you to define what you want to accomplish and what kind of life you want to have. It gives you a sense of direction and purpose and helps you to focus on the things that matter most to you. This is the "what" that helps you pinpoint the area where you want to focus your attention. Clarity helps you chart the most direct path to your goals. It will also help you determine what to say "yes" or "no" to based on your own personal values. You don't waste time or energy on things that run counter to your vision. It also helps you spot potential roadblocks before you're impacted by them. It allows you to explain your vision to others so they can understand also.

- **Motivation:** A vision inspires you to pursue your goals with passion and enthusiasm. It reminds you of your potential and your dreams while motivating you to take action and make progress. This is the "why" that becomes the fire within you that reminds you of the reason you are doing what you're doing. This is the internal motor inside of you that gives you the "juice" to go the extra mile. When you're motivated to achieve something, it gives you a reason to get up every morning and strive for something greater.

- **Resilience:** A vision enables you to cope with difficulties and setbacks. It helps you to see the bigger picture and the long-term outcomes, and it encourages you to keep going despite the obstacles and challenges. It's like looking at your situation from a panoramic view rather than a still-frame view. When we're going through a challenge, our natural tendency is to focus on that one challenge or issue. Resilience helps us "zoom out" and look at the distance we've traveled and the direction we're going, regardless of the temporary roadblock. Doing this gives us the confidence to know that if we were able to get this far, then we have the capability to go even farther. This is when we remember that these momentary challenges are not our condition but our conditioning. Resiliency helps us stay *committed* to the process so we don't give up.

- **Growth:** A vision motivates you to gain new skills, acquire fresh knowledge, and cultivate new capacities. It challenges you to stretch yourself beyond your comfort zone and to grow as a person. Even if the road is scary and makes you feel inadequate, your quest for growth will outweigh your fears because you realize the ultimate reward is greater than the perceived risk. This is where you develop the courage to move forward despite your fears. This addresses the "how" of you moving from one stage to the next.

How to Create and Pursue Your Vision

Creating and pursuing your vision is not something that happens overnight. It is a gradual process that requires reflection, imagination, planning, and action. The following steps can help you navigate this process.

Step 1: Reflect on your values, passions, and strengths. These are the things that will shape your vision and guide your actions. Your values are the principles that strongly influence your decisions and behavior. Passions are the things that you love doing and that make you happy. They're also not a burden to you. Strengths are the things that you're good at and that give you confidence. To reflect on these components, you can ask yourself questions such as: What are the things that matter most to me? What are the things that I enjoy doing and that bring me joy? What are the things that I am good at and that make me proud? The Distinction and Inspiration chapters of this book focus on taking the time to know and appreciate who you are, your strengths and weaknesses, and your unique qualities. They also focus on finding, fostering, and fueling the passion that's inside of you.

Service Road of Life

Sometimes you'll find yourself on the "service road" of life. A service road is a small road that runs parallel to a bigger, faster road. Service roads are mainly used to travel at a slower speed and access properties that border the road that cannot be reached using the fast road. They're not intended to be used by through traffic.

A service road here is a metaphor to let you know that there are times when it is necessary to slow down, catch up with yourself, reflect, and evaluate on where you've been, where you are currently in life, and where you're going. It is important to remember that even if you're on the service road, you're still moving in the same direction as the expressway, just at a slower speed. This is an important reminder for you to stay in your lane and keep moving forward. In due time, you will get back on the entrance ramp to the expressway, where the traffic becomes faster and where heightened awareness of what's happening in front of you, to the side, and behind you is essential. But know this: when you enter that expressway, you will have a lane created just for you, based on your purpose and your ability to grab hold to that purpose and not be preoccupied by someone else's lane or purpose.

Step 2: Imagine your ideal future. This is where you can unleash your creativity and dream big. Think about where you want to be in five, ten, or twenty years. What do you want to accomplish? How do you want to grow? What kind of lifestyle do you want to have? More importantly, what type of person do you want to become? Be as specific and realistic as possible, but also allow yourself to explore different possibilities and scenarios. You can use tools such as a vision board or a mind map to help you visualize your ideal future.

Where Will Your Feet Land?

Let's examine the African impala. The African impala is a medium-sized antelope found in eastern and southern Africa.

A notable fact about the African impala is that it can jump vertically over ten feet high and horizontally more than thirty feet. That is physically impressive, as it can soar to the highest heights and leap to the greatest distances. Yet even with all its impressive natural physical gifts, this magnificent creature can be kept in an enclosure in any zoo with only a three-foot wall. Why? Because they won't jump if they cannot see where their feet will land. If they can't see it, they won't do it[21].

This is an opportune time to ask a poignant question. The question is simply this: what have you made up in your mind that you will not attempt simply because you have no idea where your feet would land? Let's look at it. Mental know-how? You got it. Skill? Check. Natural ability? Check. Past evidence of accomplishment? Check. You may have been able to account for all those qualifications. The only missing variable is physically knowing, with your natural senses, where you will land should you decide to take the leap.

This is a question that encourages us to reflect on our fears and the limitations we impose on ourselves. Though it's natural to feel anxious about the unknown, it is important to remember that unless we are willing to face the unknown, we will never be able to grow and learn. It can be scary even to imagine stepping outside of our comfort zones and into uncharted territory. But that is where we have the chance to find new opportunities and experiences that can help us become better versions of ourselves.

Casting Your Vision

As you visualize your future, project how your next two to five years or five to ten years will look, because you must navigate any obstacles and roadblocks that today brings.

Dare to go to places in your mind where you've never been before. It's like you're sending your secret agents to "scope out" the mental landscape and give you a description of what it looks like. Put your deposit or "earnest money" down on that land. When you put earnest money down, it indicates your intention to one day purchase it at a future time—to own it. You're paying it off with the components of how you evolve as an individual. This will be substantiated by your growth, determination, and courage to move forward despite being uncomfortable.

What we can physically "see" is only half the story. Sight is having the ability to see what's in front of you. Vision, in the context of D.R.I.V.E., is having the ability to see *beyond* what's in front of you. When we take the time and effort to see things not just as they are today but as they have the potential to become, we can begin to prepare for this potential by making the necessary room to occupy it in our minds. It's all a matter of perspective. How you view a situation can many times determine your success or failure in that situation. For example, when we face a challenging situation, it's important to approach it with an open mind and a willingness to learn. Instead of focusing on the negative aspects, try to find opportunities for self-improvement. What's equally important to remember is that failure is not the opposite of success but rather part of the journey toward it. It's in our failures that we can learn valuable lessons and insights that help us achieve our goals in the long run.

You see, at one point or another, we all experience major change, challenge, and difficulty. Having vision does not exempt us from experiencing those things. However, when you have a vision, you can look beyond the situation confronting you and see your prize. You begin to realize that challenges and difficulties are the ingredients in the recipe for your success and fulfillment. By doing this, we can begin the process of claiming mental road space, thereby unleashing our creative and innovative capabilities to transform our lives for the better.

Dare to Dream

This has been something that I have consistently been faced with at various times in my life. I dared not only to imagine beyond what was presently in front of me but also to envision myself being where I wanted to be and doing what I wanted to do. *What often stands between our current position and where we'd like to end up is the faith to make the leap.* But before the action can be pursued in the physical realm, it must first be pursued in the mental realm. It requires having the mindset and the faith to take your mind someplace where it has never been before. It involves one daring to dream. This has always been second nature to me. At times, when it seems like I was in a barren and lonely place, faith was all I had. But then again, it was exactly what I needed.

Faith never made things easy for me, but it did make things possible. To look at me today and see the husband and father that I am to my wife and two adult sons is to see the result of faith put into action. To simply look at the early overview of my life, one would not necessarily have come to that conclusion. It would not have been probable that a child from a single-parent household, growing up in government-assisted housing, whose mother had a ninth-grade education and whose father was nowhere in the picture would have had the outcome that I've had. There was a highly probable chance that I would not graduate from high school, go on to college on a full athletic scholarship, graduate with a bachelor's degree in business, and then go onto earn my master's degree immediately following that—only to land a job at a Fortune 50 company where I worked for thirty years, buying multiple homes, getting married, having children, starting a few businesses, and being a mentor and an advisor to other men.

SPIRITUAL MARKER: As I look back at this run of major accomplishments, it was highly improbable that all of this would come to be. My environment and the statistics were not on my side. However, as my mother would often tell me, with God, *anything* is possible! Yes, that is absolutely correct. He can make the improbable possible! I stayed with God along my journey. Not that I was perfect. Lord knows I made my share of mistakes, but with those mistakes came lessons, and with those lessons came learning points, and with those learning points came growth. I stayed on my course and didn't allow the mistakes, the hard lessons, and the growing pains to turn me around. I kept moving forward, determined to turn my dreams into reality. But when improbability becomes possibility, then anything can happen!

Step 3: Write down your vision statement. This is where you summarize your vision in a concise statement that captures its essence and inspires you. A vision statement is a positive, clear, and compelling expression of your vision that answers the question: What do I want to achieve in the future, and how do I want to live my life? You can use words, phrases, or sentences to write your vision statement. For example, "I want to be a successful entrepreneur who creates innovative solutions for social problems" or "I want to live a healthy and balanced life with my family and friends." You can also search for online tools to help you craft your vision statement.

Who Will You Become?

Before an architect draws up plans for a multimillion-dollar structure that they plan to design, they first get an idea from someone who has thought about it at great length. Before an award-winning artist records a catchy record that gets lots of air play, they're first inspired by something and then move that inspiration into what they want the listeners to feel when they hear it. Just as ideas are transformed into actions, so should our intentions on who we want to become be transformed into consistent actions to achieve this.

A few years ago, prior to turning fifty years old, I took some time to think about what I wanted life to look like for myself after fifty. I began to honestly look at where I fared in certain areas compared to where I wanted to be. In doing so, I noticed some gaps. I began to write out where those gaps were and made a commitment to myself to close those gaps. In the process, I created new routines that would increase my chances of being the person I wanted to become in all the areas that I listed. That document would later become my quest for life.

When I wrote my quest for life, I did it because I wanted to create something that came from my own mouth to hold me accountable for what I was going to do going forward. Here's my quest:

My Quest for Life

To Experience a better version of Derrick D. Copeland, Sr.

This is controlled by the following:

- What I allow myself to think/believe
- What I eat
- What I allow myself to see & hear
- What I do (my activity)

My life's journey from this point on (Sunday, August 15th, 2021 @ 10:34 am CST) is to *strive* for this daily and then to take in/*experience* what this feels like, and then share my experience with others.

This will require facing and overcoming: fear, mediocrity, complacency, laziness, pride, selfishness, hurt, anger, pain, and regret.

But most importantly, it requires checking in, daily, and walking with (continuously), the one who knows what the best version of me looks like—The Almighty God!

My "Quest for Life" document is taped to my bathroom mirror, and it's also saved in my phone as a screenshot. I make it a point to read it out loud daily to not only remind myself of *what* I'm doing but *why* I'm doing it.

Step 4: Break down your vision into smaller goals. This is where you make your vision more manageable and achievable by breaking it down into smaller and more specific goals. Sometimes the most difficult thing is seeing how you will get from point A to point D. It can seem overwhelming to look that far down the road. However, when you stop to only look at how you will get from point A to point B, then point B to point C, it becomes easier to reach point D. As you focus on the steps and milestones of each point, it becomes easier to see and be encouraged about reaching your goal. Goals are the milestones that will help you move closer to your vision. For each goal, identify the actions, resources, and time frame required to accomplish it. You can use the well-known SMART criteria:

- **S**pecific—Well defined, clear, unambiguous.
- **M**easurable—Quantifying criteria to track progress toward accomplishment of the goal.
- **A**chievable—Your goals should make you stretch but remain possible to achieve.
- **R**elevant—Within reach, realistic, and relevant to your purpose and values.
- **T**ime-bound—With a clearly defined timeline, including start date and a target date, creating a sense of urgency ensuring you stay on track[22].

This will help you set effective goals. For example, "I want to launch my own business by the end of the year" or "I want to run a marathon by next year."

The Power of Choice

Anything that you aspire to do, you can do, but a big part of that will be determined by the choices that you make. As mentioned earlier, I came from very humble beginnings. However, even with those humble beginnings, I made choices early on in life that I wanted more than my immediate surroundings could provide. I made a list of the things I wanted in life and the type of person I wanted to become. This was very important for me because it ended up influencing a lot of the decisions that I would make in my life. That didn't mean that I didn't make mistakes along the way. But even with those mistakes, I had the courage to change course and get back on track. In doing so, I was able to achieve the dreams and goals that I had set for myself.

Choices are the connection between where you are and where you want to be. They're also the connection between where you are and where you don't want to be. It's our choices that will take us to either destination, and it's you who have the power to choose.

Remember, *there are many voices in your head.* You have your inner voice and then the voices of others who may doubt you or remind you of your past mistakes. Some voices have such an influence on us that they may hold us back and keep us from fulfilling our full potential. *Which one have you given permission to have the final say?* Your choices become the barometer to determine your level of commitment.

Birds of a Feather

Another important consideration when breaking down your vision into smaller goals is to ask yourself, "Who is in my life?" Also ask, "Who do I want to travel with me on this part of my journey?" and "Are they helping to maximize my potential or minimize it?" This goes back to principles we covered in chapter three, Your Relationships. The reason this becomes so important is that *your associations determine your accommodation* (they determine where you will ultimately end up residing and the quality of life you will have). As I was growing up, my mother would always tell me, "Be careful who you keep company with because birds of a feather flock together." She was telling me to be nice to everyone but give my time to those who are going in the same direction I was. This was important for me as I was growing up because the negative influences that were out there could take me down a path that I may not be able to return from, so "choose wisely," she would tell me. She helped me to be a good discerner of people. She said, "See how they treat other people. If they're talking about others behind their back, chances are they're talking about you behind your back." Another thing she would say is, "Don't hang around 'going nowhere' people." It wasn't just that they didn't have any direction, but they didn't *want* to have any direction. As I grew older, I began to see that not all people that I came across had this same message coming from their home as I had coming from mine. That's where my mother's words of being kind and nice to people and the determination and direction that I possessed in my life could quite possibly "rub off" on others, and they could emulate those qualities and strive to do better. However, there are some who have made up their minds what they're going to do (be it good or bad), and they've decided they're okay with the consequences. They're gonna do what they're gonna do. Your goals can either be realized or stalled by who you allow to travel this path with you, so choose wisely.

Step 5: Review and revise your vision regularly. This is where you monitor your progress and celebrate your achievements along the way. A vision is not a static or fixed thing. It is a dynamic and evolving process that reflects your growth and changes depending on your circumstances. Therefore, you need to review and revise your vision regularly to make sure it still aligns with your values, passions, and strengths. You also need to adjust your goals and actions accordingly, and to acknowledge your successes and learn from your failures. You can use tools such as journals or get advice from a mentor to help you review and revise your vision.

Creating a vision for your life is one of the best things you can do for yourself. A vision can help you to create the future you want and to live the life you deserve. A vision can give you clarity, motivation, resilience, and growth. It can also make you happier, more fulfilled, and more confident.

Envisioning the Road You Want to Travel

I had a dream of becoming a husband and father. I wanted to start a new generation of men and carry forth the values and ideals that I cherish so that my sons could pass it down to their children. I can say that I am currently doing that, and it feels great! It started as a mere thought, then worked its way to an idea. That idea worked its way to a plan. That plan, which is still ongoing, has turned out to be a huge blessing and is bearing much fruit. I am blessed beyond measure, and the fruit that has been produced is "being a blessing." I want to take this blessing and expand it so that it can multiply in nature. I have nurtured and watered my marriage and children, and I want the seeds that I have sown in them to produce much fruit and flourish. But I don't want them to end there; I want them to become vessels through which blessings flow and its effects become exponential in nature.

Your vision helps create the pathway to your destination. It keeps your sight set on what's ahead while your feet are firmly set in the present.

Success Comes When You MASTER THE MONOTONOUS

It's in the waiting period that we build our resiliency muscles. We go about the routines of life with a fervent but patient hope that success will come as we master our monotonous routine toward our goal. We don't just fall into success; we *prepare for it* and *expect it*! It's executing those daily, mundane tasks with maximum effort and attention to detail—those things that go unnoticed or unrecognized but are necessary to achieve success. It's taking the time to organize the calendar, plan for the next day, week, month, and year. It's taking the time to pay attention to the details. Things we're *supposed* to do but doing them well—day in and day out. It's focusing on the small things that matter the most.

It emphasizes the importance of consistency and perseverance in achieving success. It means that success is not just about doing something once or twice but doing it repeatedly and consistently over time. When you master the monotonous, you develop a habit of excellence that can help you achieve your goals. For example, if you want to become a great writer, you need to write every day, even when you don't feel like it. By mastering the monotonous task of writing every day, you develop the discipline and skill necessary to become a great writer. The same principle applies to any other field or endeavor. Success at anything requires hard work, dedication, and a willingness to do the same thing repeatedly until you get it right. So if you want to be successful, embrace the monotony and make it work for you!

Without a clear vision, you may end up drifting through life without any sense of direction or purpose. This can bring on feelings of confusion, frustration, and dissatisfaction. Having a vision gives you confidence for the future, helps you focus on the things in life you value, and ultimately leads to greater satisfaction and personal happiness. So take some time to reflect on what you want to achieve in life, and create a vision that inspires you to take the necessary action toward your goals.

CONSIDER and ASK YOURSELF:

- Vision, in the context of D.R.I.V.E., is having the ability to see beyond what's in front of you. It's the ability to see something not just as it is today, but what it has the potential to become. It serves as the road through which your goals and aspirations travel.
    - » Have you taken time to bring your passion front and center to formulate your vision? What can you see yourself doing if I dared you to imagine doing

the thing that "everyone knows you for" and for the thing that brings you fulfillment and purpose?

» What would be your aspiration? What would you make as your goal(s)? Write it down.

- When you imagine your ideal future, this is where you can unleash your creativity and dream big. Think about where you want to be in five, ten, or twenty years from now. Take a few minutes and think about what goals you would like to accomplish.

» Now that you have envisioned the person you want to become and the goals you'd like to accomplish, can you "see" yourself in that space? What would you be wearing? What would you be doing? How would you be helping or providing a service to people? Get how that looks in your mind's eye, and visit it often.

» What steps will you take to hold yourself accountable to your vision?

- You have both your inner voice and the voice of others who may doubt you or remind you of your past mistakes.

» What story is holding you back? What is making it seemingly impossible to see what your life has the potential to become?

» Will you make the choice to believe in yourself? What voices have you given permission to rule in your mind?

- What plan(s) have you put in place to support your vision? How committed have you been to carrying out your plan(s)?
    - » Will you demonstrate the power you hold to make a decision about your future?
    - » Will you allow your *why* to become bigger than any fear or doubt so you can take a new road toward what you envision?

Chapter 6: Your Evolution

Evolution (*n*): "a process of continuous change from a lower, simpler, or worse to a higher, more complex, or better state: growth." (Merriam-Webster)

> **"The journey of 1,000 miles begins with a single step."**
> —Lao Tzu

Most of us at some point or another in our lives have heard the expression "where the rubber meets the road." It's a colloquial expression that means the most important point for something, or the moment of truth, where a theory, idea, or someone's efforts are put to the test. As we used to say growing up where I come from, it's time to "put up or shut up!"

In the context of D.R.I.V.E., evolution is the gear where that visionary faith is put into motion and gains traction, moving you from one point to the next. It's in movement where progress is made.

Oliver Wendell Holmes said, "I find the great thing in this world is not so much where we stand, as in what direction we are moving." He goes on to say, "We must sail sometimes with the wind and sometimes against it—but we must sail, and not drift, nor lie at anchor." His statement underscores the basis on which the "evolution" gear stands. That it's not enough to just know where you are and have a sense of where you're going; you must also know in what direction you are moving. The direction of our movement is just as important, if not more important, than our movement itself. For movement with no specific direction is merely motion.

The word "evolve" means "to develop gradually, especially from a simple to a more complex form." We should always look to evolve, make progress, advance, move forward, mature, transform, adapt, unfold into all that we were created to be. To do this, we must be willing to move outside of our comfort zones and understand that we live in a constantly changing world, but even with those changes, we have elasticity inside of us to handle us taking different forms. Many times, it's hard for people to see their older, mature, advanced, transformed selves. We hold onto the familiar and shy away from the unfamiliar.

SPIRITUAL MARKER: When our hope intersects with our faith, this is where we begin to walk it out through our actions. Because God knows our ending from our beginning, we can trust that when we pair our sincere effort with his divine destiny, our "good" will be produced. Jeremiah 29:11 (NIV) says, "For I know the plans I have for you, declares the Lord, plans to prosper you and not to harm you, plans to give you hope and a future."

If we don't have the courage to evolve and accept our "new thing" rather than our "former thing," then we end up approaching the road looking into the rearview mirror rather than looking through the front windshield with our eyes fixed on the road ahead.

Personal growth is a lifelong process that involves developing new habits, changing old ones, and overcoming obstacles. It is a journey that requires patience, perseverance, and self-reflection. Personal growth is not a one-time event but rather a continuous process of learning and self-improvement. It involves stepping out of your comfort zone, taking risks, and embracing change. Developing new habits is an essential part of personal growth. It requires discipline, consistency, and a willingness to try new things. *Changing old habits can be challenging, but it is necessary for personal growth.* Overcoming obstacles is also an integral part of the process. Obstacles can be viewed as opportunities for growth and learning. They can help you develop resilience, strength, and character. Personal growth is a journey that requires effort, but the rewards are immeasurable. It can lead to greater self-awareness, improved relationships, and a more fulfilling life.

In this chapter, we explore the role habits play in our lives, the development of healthy habits, and how embracing change helps us in our personal growth journey.

Understanding Habits and Their Role in Personal Growth

Habits are things we do regularly and automatically, often without even thinking about them. They can be good or bad for us, depending on what they are. Habits can be hard to change because we do them so often, but we can also choose to make new habits or stop doing old ones if we want. By doing this, we can improve ourselves and live a happier, healthier, and more fulfilling life.

Good habits are essential for personal growth and well-being. They can have a significant impact on our physical and mental well-being and help us achieve our goals. For instance, making a habit of exercising regularly can help us maintain a healthy weight, reduce the risk of chronic diseases, and boost our mood. Conversely, bad habits such as smoking, excessive drinking, or procrastination can have detrimental effects on our health, relationships, and productivity.

Personal growth is about improving oneself through learning, self-reflection, and self-awareness. Habits are a crucial part of this process because they can help us develop new skills, change our mindset, and achieve our goals. By cultivating good habits and eliminating bad ones, we can create a positive environment for personal growth and development.

Habits are the result of choices that we make in any given area of our lives. Whether we've established good or bad reasons for the habit, we live with the results. If we want different results, we must change the choices that lead to those habits. As mentioned earlier, choices are the connection between where you are and where you *want* to be. They're also the connection between where you are and where you *don't* want to be. Your choices are what will take you to either destination, and you are the one who has the power to choose.

Oftentimes, we experience one of two pains in life: the pain of discipline or the pain of regret. It is ours to choose. The hard choices you make today will save you from a lot of hardships down the road. We can either endure the temporary pain associated with the struggle of striving for something we've never achieved before or experience the unsettling pain of regret that comes from having never tried. You don't get through life without pain at some points at the very least. That is an inevitable fact. As stated earlier in the chapter, you can't stay where you are and get to where you want to be at the same time. It is an impossible feat. But even with the impossibilities that exist with this quest, many of us attempt to do this—with the expectation that it should happen. We will even get upset when it doesn't come to pass. Just because we want something really badly, however, that doesn't mean we deserve it. Only when we're willing to put the necessary time, energy, and intentional effort into something will we get something out of it.

In chapter four, Inspiration, I talked about the importance of establishing your *why*. In your life's journey, your *why* becomes your reason for doing what you do. It's what will make the person who wants to stop smoking, lose the weight, or earn the degree do the work to get to their goal. That's because the win is not just for today but for the benefit they will see down the road.

Developing Good Habits and Breaking Bad Ones

Developing good habits and breaking bad ones can be challenging, but they are not impossible. According to a *Forbes* article[23], habits are routines of behavior that are repeated regularly and tend to occur subconsciously. They can be created by physiological exposure that shows itself in regularity. However, not all habits are created equal. Some habits can be beneficial, while others can be detrimental to our well-being. Here are some tips to help you develop good habits and break bad ones:

1. **Identify your triggers**. Identifying the triggers that lead to your bad habits is the first step in breaking them. Once you know the prompts that trigger your bad habits, you can take steps to avoid them.

2. **Replace bad habits with good ones**. Instead of trying to eliminate bad habits, try replacing them with good ones. For example, if you have a habit of snacking on junk food, replace the junk food with a healthier snack like fruits or nuts.

3. **Start small**. Trying to change too much too quickly can be overwhelming. Start with small changes and gradually work your way up.

4. **Track your progress**. Keeping track of your progress can help you stay motivated. Use a habit tracker to monitor your progress and celebrate your successes.

5. **Stay positive**. Developing good habits and breaking bad ones can be challenging, but it's important to stay positive. Focus on your successes and don't beat yourself up over your failures.

Remember, developing good habits takes time and effort, but it's worth it in the end.

Zig Ziglar said, "When you choose a habit, you choose the results of that habit." Keep that in mind when you are establishing new habits and putting them into play. This is where we learn how to adapt and become our true selves, for it is essential to embrace authenticity and growth.

Take advantage of every moment you have. Always take steps that drive you toward, not away from, your goals. Exchange those habits that prohibit you from reaching your potential and replace them with habits that will catapult you toward them. Always keep the big picture in mind, and know that every day brings with it another opportunity.

Knowing who you are and what you are connected to is another important part of developing your habits. When you know this, you can acknowledge those things deep inside of you, take action (first seeing things as they can become), and then do the hard things of putting new thinking and habits into motion to create a better version of yourself. This is where you lean into growth and development and fight the temptation to resist it, keeping a posture of learning and inquiry rather than inflexibility and stagnation.

The Importance of Changing

Noted author, speaker, and longtime leadership guru John Maxwell says, "Change is inevitable. Growth is optional."

Change is an inevitable part of life that can be difficult to accept. However, it is essential for personal growth. Change introduces you to new experiences, challenges, and opportunities that can help you learn and grow. It can help you overcome difficulties and develop new skills. By embracing change, you can become more adaptable, resilient, and open-minded. As Albert Einstein once said, "The world as we have created it is a process of our thinking. It cannot be changed without changing our thinking."

Change can also help you break free from negative patterns and habits that may be holding you back. It can help you gain a fresh perspective on life and discover new passions and interests. By stepping out of your comfort zone and trying new things, you can expand your horizons and discover new aspects of yourself.

In summary, change is essential for personal growth because it helps you learn, grow, and become a better version of yourself. By embracing change, you can overcome challenges, develop new skills, and discover new passions and interests. Remember, change is not always easy, but it is necessary for growth and progress.

A hugely important factor in our ability to evolve and develop into better versions of ourselves is how we respond to change. In his book *The Principles and Benefits of Change: Fulfilling Your Purpose in Unsettled Times*, Myles Munroe talks about four distinct types of change in life:

1. **Change that happens *to us*** — unexpected or anticipated change that affects our personal lives, families, careers, and so forth

2. **Change that happens *around us*** — unexpected or anticipated change that affects our society, nation, or world and that also has some impact on us personally or on our ways of life

3. **Change that happens *within us*** — unexpected or anticipated change that directly affects who we are either physically, emotionally, mentally, or spiritually

4. **Change that we *initiate*** — something created or altered by plans we have implemented to move us from the present to a preferred future[24]

Along your journey in life, there will be signs to let you know that change is necessary. The question is whether you will heed the road signs in your life. You decide to either obey them or ignore them, but they will make themselves known. It is better to obey the signs and deal with the change when there is adequate distance between them and you have time to ease into the transition rather than ignore them and wait until there is no time to transition. The hard slap of reality might not be pleasant.

To illustrate this further, the phrase "Use Caution: Bridge May Be Icy" is a warning sign commonly seen in areas prone to cold weather and snow. The "Use Caution" part of the sign advises people to be careful and exercise vigilance. It's a reminder to proceed with awareness to and take necessary precautions. The "Bridge May Be Icy" part specifies the reason for the caution. It indicates the bridge surface could be slippery due to ice. When temperatures drop, bridges tend to freeze faster than regular roads because they are exposed on all sides, including from below. The sign is urging everyone to be mindful and adjust their behavior when crossing the bridge, especially during icy conditions. It's a safety measure to prevent accidents and slips. Similar to that example, when we heed the warnings signs in our lives and utilize the time afforded to us to make adjustments (our window of opportunity), we stand a higher chance of safeguarding ourselves and preventing unfortunate outcomes.

Many times, it seems easiest to take the path of least resistance. However, this path comes with a price. The price is not always apparent up front but becomes glaringly apparent when the time comes due. The price we pay for ease might not be monetary but could manifest itself in lost potential, unexplored paths, and the haunting question "What if?"

Your ability to not only expect but also accept change as a necessity to grow and develop is critical. Equally important is your willingness and courage to say goodbye to the old and hello to the new. How you manage these transitions and new realities in your life will determine whether you evolve or just exist.

How Are You Changing and Growing?

What is your willingness to change and grow? Your willingness or resistance to change will determine your progress or stagnation. No one is too young, and no one is too old, to grow and develop.

The world around us and its advancement, from even the most primitive times to the information age where we now find ourselves, has seen its necessary times and seasons, and this pattern will continue. To everything there is a season, and a time to every purpose[25]. We as humans are meant to transform and evolve—to grow, mature, and develop. However, we can become so accustomed to the comfort of the cocoon that we tell ourselves a story to make us "feel" good even though we're not progressing. *If we're not careful, we can mistakenly allow our feelings to become the barometer for growth and development.* Growth is that continuous process that requires commitment, effort, and reflection.

There is a "press" that comes with evolving and growing into better, more advanced forms of ourselves. The press is not only a physical press but a mental press as well—a constant transformation of removing and replenishing. We must continually flush out the remnants of toxic thoughts, experiences, and emotions, while at the same time we reach for tangible things that will satisfy our need for accomplishment. This is not an easy process, but it is tremendously worth it because we can grow in ways we had never imagined, which makes it more realistic for us to be in a healthier state of mind as we work toward our goals. Keep pressing forward[26].

In our life's journey, there will be times of pain and struggle. We can either live with the pain of the struggle to strive for something we've never achieved before, or we can endure the pain of regret that comes from never having tried. You can't stay where you are and get to where you want to be at the same time. You must be willing, intentional, and educated, and you must execute like your life depends on it. Because in actuality, the quality of your life does depend on your ability to make the necessary changes to advance to the next stage of your development. If we do the things we've always done, we'll get the things we've always gotten. To get what we've never gotten before, we must do what we've never done before. That extends to thinking the way we've never thought before. Change, growth, and development are the seeds we plant in the soil of our lives that we hope will grow and one day provide a comfortable shade.

Take the time to learn new things and strip away old mindsets. What worked ten years, five years, or even one year ago might not work today. Adapt to the world as it is today. This is a revealing time, as it reveals your preparation or lack thereof. It reveals your readiness, what's important to you, and your ability to focus. Our lives change, and we are built to evolve. Consider the caterpillar's transformation into a butterfly. That is a natural evolution; whether the caterpillar wants to transform or not, it *will* transform.

As we get older, discipline becomes more important. For growth, it will be paramount. Situations change, and scenes change, like the backdrop of a stage play. This requires us to change with them, or else we'll be playing a role that is no longer relevant to the situation. This will render us ineffective, and we'll experience frustration because we're unable to operate in the new environment or reality.

How to Embrace Change and Overcome Resistance to It

Change can be tough to accept, but it is necessary for personal and professional growth. According to an article in the *Harvard Business Review*, many people unconsciously believe that change is temporary. But when you view change as temporary, you're more likely to cope with it instead of embracing it. The truth is that change is a constant, and you'll need to navigate it frequently in both your career and personal life.

Dealing with resistance to change can be challenging. However, there are some steps you can take to make the process smoother.

- First, it's important to acknowledge the resistance and identify the benefits of the change.
- Educate yourself about the change to best understand the reasons, benefits, and impacts of the change.
- Then, take small steps and surround yourself with supportive people.
- Staying positive is also key in keeping a growth mindset[27].

Another way to reduce resistance to change is to communicate why the change is happening and reassure people as much as possible. Addressing their underlying concerns can also help.

Remember, change is inevitable. But instead of fearing it, we can embrace it as an opportunity to learn and grow. By consciously examining how we approach change, we can adopt strategies to move toward a more change-ready mindset. When we do this, we can welcome change as an opportunity to learn and grow.

Addition by Subtraction

It is often said that to add something of significance to your life, you must first subtract things that are not serving you. This can be a difficult process, but it is necessary to make room for the best available option for you in that season. By removing things from your life and from your daily agenda that are not adding value, you create space for new opportunities and experiences. This can be as simple as decluttering your home or as complex as ending a toxic relationship. Whatever the case may be, it is important to remember that subtraction is not a punishment but rather a way to make room for growth and change. As you subtract things from your life, you will begin to see the benefits of living with less and the positive impact it can have on your overall well-being.

Now I'm going to say something that may appear to go against what I have been suggesting throughout the book, which is that growth and development are all about moving forward. In essence, that is true. However, there are times when it becomes necessary to step back (or sideways) to grow. For this, we must accept the fact that personal growth is not always linear or upward. Sometimes our growth and development come when we've moved down or across a learning curve to reach a new level of understanding, performance, or potential. This might involve taking a risk, making a sacrifice, or facing a failure, but it can also lead to a breakthrough or a transformation. For example, imagine a person who has been working in the same job for several years. They have been doing well and have even been promoted a few times. However, they feel like they're not learning anything new and are not being challenged enough. As a result, they start to feel stuck and unfulfilled. In this scenario, this person realizes they need to step back or sideways in order to grow. They decide to take a lateral move to gain some additional skills that may be outside of their comfort zone. This new opportunity may not be as prestigious as their previous job, but it offers them a chance to learn new skills and, in turn, become a more valuable asset.

By taking a calculated detour, the person can grow in ways that they would not have been able to if they had stayed in their old job. They learn new things, meet new people, and gain a fresh perspective. This experience helps them to become a more well-rounded and fulfilled person.

How Obstacles Can Be Opportunities for Growth

Obstacles are often viewed as negative experiences that hinder progress. However, they can come our way for many reasons. Some of those reasons are:

- **To test our abilities**. They can be a way to test our abilities and see how far we can go.

- **To teach us a lesson**. They can help us learn from our mistakes and see things from a new perspective.

- **To help us grow**. They can help us develop new skills, learn new things, and become better individuals.

- **To help us appreciate what we have**. They can help us realize the value of things that we may take for granted.

- **To help us become more resilient**. They can help us develop the ability to bounce back from difficult situations.

- **To help us become more creative**. They can help us think outside the box and come up with new solutions to problems.
- **To help us become more persistent**. They can help us develop the ability to keep going even when things get tough.
- **To help us become more patient**. They can help us learn to wait for things and not give up too easily.
- **To help us become more empathetic**. They can help us understand the struggles of others and become more compassionate.

Because we can experience obstacles for many different reasons, it is important to approach it with a positive mindset and view it as a chance to learn and improve.

One way to turn obstacles into opportunities is to reframe the situation. Instead of focusing on the negative aspects of the obstacle, try to identify the potential benefits. For example, if you are struggling to complete a project, you could view it as an opportunity to develop your problem-solving skills and learn new techniques.

Another way to approach obstacles is to use them as a chance to reflect on your strengths and weaknesses. By analyzing how you respond to challenges, you can identify areas where you need to improve and develop strategies to overcome them. This can help you build resilience and become more adaptable in the face of adversity.

Finally, obstacles can be opportunities to learn from others. Seeking advice and guidance from others who have faced similar challenges can provide valuable insights and help you develop new skills. Additionally, working collaboratively with others can help you build stronger relationships and develop a support network that can help you overcome future obstacles.

In conclusion, obstacles can be viewed as opportunities for growth and development. By approaching them with a positive mindset, reframing the situation, reflecting on your strengths and weaknesses, and learning from others, you can turn obstacles into opportunities for personal and professional growth.

Examples of How to Overcome Obstacles and Grow from Them

Overcoming obstacles can be a challenging task, but it is essential for personal growth and development. Here are some tips to help you overcome obstacles and grow from them:

1. **Identify the obstacle**: The first step in overcoming an obstacle is to identify it. Take some time to reflect on the situation and understand what is holding you back.

2. **Create a plan**: Once you have identified the obstacle, create a plan to overcome it. Break down the problem into smaller, more manageable steps, and set achievable goals.

3. **Stay positive**: It's easy to get discouraged when facing obstacles, but it's important to stay positive. Focus on your strengths and accomplishments and use them to motivate yourself.

4. **Learn from your mistakes:** Obstacles are an opportunity to learn and grow. Take the time to reflect on what went wrong and use that knowledge to avoid making the same mistakes in the future.

5. **Ask for help**: Don't be afraid to ask for help when you need it. Reach out to friends, family, colleagues or in some cases that may require it, a professional for support and guidance.

Remember, overcoming obstacles takes time and effort, but it is worth it in the end. By following these tips, you can overcome any obstacle and grow from the experience.

How to Develop Yourself in Various Areas

Developing oneself is a continuous process that requires consistent effort and dedication. Here are some tips to help you develop yourself in various areas:

1. **Physical development**: Regular exercise, healthy eating habits, and sufficient sleep are essential for physical development. You can also consider taking up a new sport or activity to challenge yourself physically.

2. **Mental development**: Reading books, learning new skills, and engaging in intellectual discussions can help you develop mentally. You can also try prayer, meditation, or mindfulness practices to improve your focus and concentration.

3. **Emotional development**: Developing emotional intelligence, practicing empathy, and building healthy relationships can help you develop emotionally. You can also try journaling or therapy to improve your emotional well-being.

4. **Social development**: Building a strong social network, volunteering, and engaging in community activities can

help you develop socially. You can also try attending networking events or joining clubs to meet new people.

5. **Spiritual development**: Practicing gratitude, prayer, and meditation can help you develop spiritually and can serve as an anchor during challenging times.

Remember, developing oneself is a personal journey, and it's important to find what works best for you. Start small, set achievable goals, and be patient with yourself. With consistent effort, you can achieve your personal development goals and become a better version of yourself.

Remember that change is not often easy; in fact, most times it's hard, depending on the extent and the pace of change we experience. But it's necessary for growth. Keep pushing yourself out of your comfort zone, and you'll be amazed at how you can evolve and what you can achieve.

When we get to a place where we have grown and developed into a better form of ourselves, we must reintroduce ourselves to our improved selves. When we do this, we have acknowledged and appreciated our own growth and progress. There is a quote by the famous poet Rumi: "Yesterday I was clever, so I wanted to change the world. Today I am wise, so I am changing myself." It is important to take the time to reflect on our journey and appreciate how far we've come. It's also important to set new goals and aspirations for ourselves and to work toward achieving them. By doing so, we can continue to grow and evolve into even better versions of ourselves.

Though there are issues and problems in the world today, there are also opportunities that abound, swirling around in the atmosphere, just waiting for a place to land—waiting for good ground to fall on. When we evolve, we put ourselves in a position to have those opportunities land squarely on us. *There are opportunities waiting to land. The question is: Will you be a suitable landing spot?*

Know Your Moment!

Play the game of life to win. Don't play not to lose. Shift yourself into drive rather than driving in neutral, hoping a strong wind or downhill slope will give you momentum. Your "momentum" comes when you're comfortable with *who* you are, when you know *why* you're here, and when you know *where* you're going.

There will be times when you'll have to revisit knowing and appreciating who you are, having a community around you that is feeding and cultivating you and not sucking energy from you. You must never forget your *why*, so that you don't lose your way and so you continue to have faith in the vision you saw for yourself. We are continually in the process of becoming. Who we've been, who we are, and who we hope to become is a process of choosing faith over fear, which will help us to put one foot in front of the other. The goal is to leave everything out on the field of life. Your evolution pours into the legacy you will leave behind. It allows your vision, hard work, and actions to reach far beyond today.

Whatever season you find yourself in, know that you were meant for that season, and that season was meant for you. Don't shirk your season. Complete it and learn from it. Allow it to prepare you for your next season. As we transition from one season to the next, our mindsets and actions must evolve, just like the transitions that occur in the environment. When we're able to accept and evolve with these cycles of life, we become able to move through our life's journey more easily, knowing that our circumstances are always temporary.

CONSIDER and ASK YOURSELF:

- Habits are the result of choices that we make in any given area of our lives. Whether we've established good or bad reasons for the habit, we live with the results.

    » What results have you previously "lived with" because you weren't willing to change your habits?

    » Which habits are you willing (and ready) to change so that you can live the life that you really want to live?

- By removing things from your life and from your daily agenda that are not adding value, you create space for new opportunities and experiences.

    » What one or two things are you willing to remove from your daily (or weekly) agenda to create space for new opportunities?

    » What will you do to replace old self-defeating habits with new healthy habits, thereby creating a new pattern that leads to a greater likelihood of success?

- You must never forget your *why* so that you don't lose your way. Continue to have faith in the vision you saw for yourself.

    » What are two ways you will keep your *why* in front of you so you can visit it daily or weekly?

    » How will you use that to help direct your decisions and guide you on how you spend your time?

- Your evolution pours into the legacy you will leave behind. It allows your vision, hard work, and actions to reach far beyond today.
    - » What are you leaving behind to let others know you were not only here, but you left an imprint on the lives of those you came into contact with?

Chapter 7:
It's Your Time—It's Time to D.R.I.V.E.!

Each one of us has a story. A story that is marked with both triumph and defeat. Some of us have stories we'd rather forget and run away from, leaving behind the unwanted memories that come with it. *Don't run from your story, but embark on the quest to unravel its meaning.* This can help you place each and every piece of your life's puzzle on the puzzle board so that you can be and do what you were created to do. Though your story may have both good and bad parts to it, it fits onto your puzzle board to make it complete and gives it meaning.

SPIRITUAL MARKER: My mother would always tell me, "Derrick, there's a time and a season for everything under the sun. Nothing happens before its appointed time, and when it's your time, there's nothing that anyone will be able to take from you. You will be able to walk right through, because you were able to make it to your season." She would also tell me, "If you haven't experienced it yet, keep living." I appreciate those words my mother gave me, because she was preparing me for life and the seasons that come with it. She taught me to keep God as my constant source of hope, joy, peace, and love—to run after him because he could make sense of my life.

This is the greatest time to be alive if you're growing, learning, and developing valuable skills. Continuously improve yourself so you become more valuable. Put new goals and habits in place and practice them. Time is our greatest and most valuable resource, for in it is our field of play to perform our life's work. Don't waste it! Why? Because it can't be given back to us. Each breath that we take and each step we take is recorded in the history of time. So be intentional. As you begin this new part of your journey, use this time just as you would spend time on a road test. You practice, you take your time as you execute, and you become alert and aware of your new surroundings to get more familiarity with this new role you have. You're behind the wheel, so it's time to consistently get your drive-time hours in—and practice!

The Importance of Practice

Practice is key to improving your skills. Just as doctors refine their expertise through continuous practice, people in all fields can benefit from it. Whether you're trying to master an instrument, perfect a song, or excel in a sport, consistent effort and repetition can help you get better. Remember, practice, like choices, is like a bridge that connects where you are to where you want to be. So keep at it!

Deliberate practice is a power tool for overcoming obstacles and achieving success. When we take the time to focus on specific areas of improvement and work systematically to address them, we can develop the skills we need to achieve our goals.

The Practice Paradox

But what if we shift our perspective? Rather than obsessing over perfection, let's focus on the practice itself. The paradox is that practice doesn't make perfect; it makes progress. Every repetition, every mistake contributes to growth. It's not about achieving an impossible goal; it's about the journey—the small steps we take toward mastery. Consider a person who wants to learn how to play the guitar. Instead of focusing on playing the perfect melody, they focus on practicing every day. They start with simple chords and gradually move on to more complex ones. They make mistakes, but they don't get discouraged. They keep practicing, and with each repetition, they get better. They realize that it's not about achieving perfection; it's about the journey of learning and growing. Eventually they become proficient at playing the guitar, not because they were obsessed with perfection but because they focused on the practice itself and enjoyed the journey.

The same principle applies to other areas of life as well. Whether it's learning a new skill, overcoming a challenge, or achieving a goal, focusing on the practice itself and enjoying the journey can lead to growth and progress. So don't be afraid to make mistakes; embrace them and keep practicing. You will be amazed at how far you can go with small step toward mastery.

The Art of Deliberate Practice

Psychologist Anders Ericsson introduced the concept of "deliberate practice." It's not mindless repetition; it's purposeful, focused effort. Deliberate practice involves breaking down skills, identifying weaknesses, and addressing them systematically. It's the pianist playing scales, the athlete refining their form, the writer revising drafts. Mastery emerges not from blind repetition but from deliberate refinement.

Being very intentional with what you focus on will continue to move you toward your goal. It's going to keep you at your center.

Embrace Imperfection

Suppose you're learning to play the guitar. You've been practicing for a few weeks, and you're still struggling to play a song without making mistakes. You feel frustrated and discouraged, and you're tempted to give up.

But instead of giving up, you decide to embrace imperfection as a companion on your journey. You realize that every missed note is an opportunity to learn and grow. You start to celebrate the flawed notes, the missed shots, and the rough drafts, recognizing that they're stepping stones on the path to mastery.

You practice with intention, focusing on the areas where you need improvement. You learn from your failures, analyzing what went wrong and how you can do better next time. And you evolve, gradually improving your skills and building your confidence.

Through this process, you discover that it's not just about reaching the destination; it's about the exhilarating journey along the way. As a result, you learn to enjoy the process of learning and growing, embracing the ups and downs as part of the adventure.

Remember, embracing imperfection doesn't mean you're settling for mediocrity. It means recognizing that perfection may remain elusive, but growth is tangible. When you practice with intention, learn from your failures, and courageously evolve, you can overcome obstacles and achieve your goals.

What Is Your Fuel?

The person you'll be in the future is based on everything you do today. The individuals you hang around with, the social media you follow, the opinions you believe, the shows you watch, and the books you read influence your future. All the information you take in, positive or negative, will affect your future. The foods you eat today will affect your future, both on a visual and an energy level. The same is true of your thoughts and information. What you feed your mind will shape your future. Your future self is pleading with you to show some discipline. Your future self is pleading with you to not be like the rest who may let fear or complacency hold them back from a more fulfilling future. If you want health and fitness, put in the work and time to get it. If you want peace and happiness, put in the work and time to get it. *Your actions will equal your results!* You're still reading this book up to this point, and that tells me that you want it. Well, guess what? Go for it! Don't let fear of the unknown or doubts about your circumstances stop you. Be who you were created to be. Do what you were created to do. And know what you were created to know. *On the other side of your biggest challenge lies your greatest opportunity.* That is both scary and exciting at the same time. But know this, you were built for both—the struggle of the challenge *and* the victory of the opportunity.

In the 2018 Marvel movie *Black Panther*, there is a gripping scene that introduces the "Show Them Who You Are!" philosophy. At some point in time, everyone must "be who they are" in this world. You first must *know* who you are, and then go out and *be* it in your everyday life. In this ritual combat scene, Prince T'Challa is fighting M'baku, who early on has the upper hand on the prince. In a desperate plea to her son, Queen Mother Ramonda says, "Show him who you are!" That statement instantly reminds him of the days that he spent with his earthly father showing him who he is and modeling what it is to be a king. All of those things hit him right between the eyes and infuse in him a renewed sense of strength, power, and identity. He then declares to his opponent who he is: "I am Prince T'Challa, son of King T'Chaka." He then begins to act out who his father told him he was and how that encompasses being the superior warrior—the Black Panther. Similar to that, there are times when we need a "show them who you are" moment. We must first remind ourselves of who we are and what we possess. We must then speak to our obstacle and tell it who we are and whose we are, and then begin to pursue with passion what and who we were created to be, being and carrying out whatever the moment demands.

Each one of us has a yearning, a craving on the inside to be satisfied. Many times, we go our whole lives in search of that thing that will make us whole. I want you to recognize that no amount of wealth, prestige, or increasing abundance will ever satisfy the human soul. Will you focus? Will you be disciplined? Will you challenge yourself to know who you are and who you were created to be so you can carry out your life's work and make the world a better place because of it?

SPIRITUAL MARKER: I have found that I am uniquely created to worship God alone. Apart from him, nothing else can bring true and lasting peace and satisfaction. God has a GPS tracking system built inside of each of us, and he will find us right where we are. All we have to do is put out the call. I can tell you without a shadow of a doubt that this journey that I have traveled and the challenges that I have dared to take on has worked (and is continuing to work) for me. I came to God hurting and confused, and now I find myself healed, and I have a strong sense of clarity—so much so that I want to experience more of him. The same hunger and passion that I had as a fifteen-year-old, growing up in the inner city and striving to find something, is the passion I have as a 50-plus-year-old man who is nestled in the comfortable suburbs of Dallas, Texas. I need God just as much, if not more, today, because I want to experience more of what he had in mind when he created me.

My "fuel" from high school to about the age of twenty-seven was pain. It was pain/hurt/discouragement, disguised as die-hard motivation, that was driving me to achieve things that had never been modeled for me and to push myself hard to improve myself. I had finally come to a point of reckoning. I came to a point where I was able to uncover internal stories that drove me because I would ultimately live out the narrative that I would tell myself. Those internal narratives we tell ourselves are interwoven and will attach themselves to become part of our identity. And so this is where our restructuring begins—with our identity. Who you believe you are ultimately drives everything.

The Challenge

Forgetting those things that are behind us and pressing forward to those things that are ahead of us is the challenge we all must continually navigate. It becomes increasingly important for this to occur if we expect to get to our destination. You can't get to where you want to go looking in the rearview mirror. Yes, there are those times when we must look at our past to face certain hurts or pains that we've experienced to overcome them, but once that has been done, we must live in the present with the hope of what's ahead. Not focusing on past mistakes, past hurts, or past decisions. Trust that the path that you're on is tailor made for you. Trust that it is one that sends you on a trajectory into your destiny. There is a "you" out there that you haven't seen yet. The daily goal is to see it, touch it, feel it, experience it.

Always ask yourself, "Who am I becoming?" None of us knows what the future holds, but we each play an active role in shaping it. Who you're becoming is more significant than what you're currently doing, for the nature of your being will shape the quality of your actions. Simply put, *who you are on the inside drives what you do on the outside.*

SPIRITUAL MARKER: I've found much success in taking heavenly principles and applying them to my earthly experience.

Many people find these things to be outdated in today's world, but I've found that all of the issues we deal with in life are addressed in biblical principles, and they have worked. My sincere desire is that you learn of God and his way. When we apply heaven's perspective to today's realities, we can solve things in the way they should be solved. Then we can become fully whole, fully complete, lacking nothing. It's about you getting closer to God's perfect plan for your life. Success is the continuing achievement of becoming the person God wants you to be and accomplishing the goals he has helped you set.

So what's it going to be? Will you commit to living life to its fullest, or will you merely exist? Your success may not be running a Fortune 500 company or striking it rich with the next big invention, but it may be getting incrementally better every day and going to bed knowing that you reached for something and, even though you may not have taken a hold of it, you got closer than you were the day before. That is success: having the *courage* to ask the question, "Where am I?"; having the *humility* to acknowledge there are some things that you need to change to become better; and having the *faith* to evolve (to grow and develop) into what you were meant to be.

Every single one of us has obstacles. The question is whether we will overcome them. Every one of us has a purpose. The question is whether we will discover it. And every one of us, at some point or another, has had a dream. The only question is whether we will pursue it. One of the most common regrets of the dying is that they wish they'd had the courage to live a life true to themselves, not the life others expected of them. Together, the motivational speakers Les Brown and the late Myles Munroe said, "The graveyard is the richest place on earth, because it is here that you will find all the hopes and dreams that were never fulfilled, the books that were never written, the songs that were never sung, the inventions that were never shared, the cures that were never discovered, all because someone was too afraid to take that first step, keep with the problem, or determined to carry out their dream."

Remember, you are uniquely qualified to be you. The goal is to be the best "you" that you can be, and every day you have an opportunity to get better at it. Take advantage of the opportunity that is before you.

My hope is that the "fuel" that's driving you is faith (rather than fear), hope (rather than doubt), and love (rather than negativity), and that it will land you in your place of destiny, so you will be who you were created to be and do what you were created to do in this world.

As I reflect on that snowy, winter day back in 1984 when my world, as I knew it, was turned upside down and I found myself broken from the outside in, I realize that I would later come to find out this was the start of the transformation that would build me up from the inside out.

My desire is that this book has awakened a greater awareness of yourself and your relationships—that it has created an authentic acknowledgment and recognition of your passion and purpose, evoking a resounding call to action by having a vision to see your life not just as it is today but what you hope for it to become. Finally, I hope it has given you the courage to take action by committing to the rewarding process of personal growth and development. My friend, this is D.R.I.V.E.—the Journey of You.

ABOUT THE AUTHOR

Derrick Copeland Sr., MA, is an author and speaker who uses life-learned lessons to captivate his readers and audiences to help them discover their purpose and pursue their dreams. Derrick strives to build individuals up from the inside out and equip them to gain an understanding of who they are so they can discover their unique abilities and their purpose. Derrick's background in sports and thirty years in corporate America have allowed him to dream big and achieve success personally and professionally. His diverse messages reach a variety of audiences, including community, academic, sports, faith-based, and corporate audiences. Derrick and his wife, Yolanda, reside in Frisco, Texas, and have two adult children, Donovan and Derrick Jr.

For more information on Derrick,
check out www.thejourneyprinciple.com.

ENDNOTES

1 Psalms 27:10—"Though my father and mother forsake me, the Lord will receive me." (The Holy Bible; NIV)

2 Isaiah 43:1—"But now, this is what I the Lord says—he who created you, Jacob, he who formed you, Israel; 'Do not fear, for I have redeemed you; I have called you by name; you are mine.'" (The Holy Bible; NIV)

3 Joshua 1:9—"Have I not commanded you? Be strong and courageous. Do not be afraid; do not be discouraged, for the Lord your God will be with you wherever you go." (The Holy Bible; NIV)

4 "Tony Robbins 6 Key Principles for Finding Your True Identity—Addicted 2 Success," July 30, 2013, by Joel Brown (Founder of Addicted2Success.com).

5 "The Mirror Test for Babies Reveals When the Self Emerges," PsyBlog (spring.org.uk), December 28, 2022, by Jeremy Dean (Child Psychology).

6 Psalms 139:14—"I praise you because I am fearfully and wonderfully made; your works are wonderful, I know that full well." (The Holy Bible; NIV)

7 Romans 12:2—"Do not conform to the pattern of this world, but be transformed by the renewing of your mind. Then you will be able to test and approve what God's will is—his good, pleasing and perfect will." (The Holy Bible; NIV)

8 Proverbs 4:23–27—"Above all else, guard your heart, for everything you do flows from it. Keep your mouth free of perversity; keep corrupt talk far from your lips. Let your eyes look straight ahead; fix your gaze directly before you. Give careful thought to the paths for your feet and be steadfast in all your ways. Do not turn to the right or the left; keep your foot from evil." (The Holy Bible; NIV)

9 1 Samuel 30:6—"David was greatly distressed because the men were talking of stoning him; each one was bitter in spirit because of his sons and daughters. But David encouraged himself in the Lord his God." (The Holy Bible; NIV)

10 *Relational Intelligence (The People Skills You Need For the Life of Purpose You Want)*, by Dr. Dharius Daniels, page 15.

11 "5 Types of Interpersonal Relationships and Why They Are Important," marriage.com, by Rachel Pace. Updated February 13, 2023.

12 "Interpersonal Relationships: Tips for How to Maintain Them," verywellmind.com, by Kendra Cherry, MSEd. Updated on April 14, 2023. Medically reviewed by Rachel Goldman, PhD, FTOS.

13 "What Is a Car Diagnostic Test?" jdpower.com, by Dustin Hawley; February 26, 2021.

14 Proverbs 18:16—"A man's gift makes room for him and brings him before great men." (The Holy Bible; KJV)

15 "Fear" (definition), Merriam-Webster

16 "F.E.A.R.—False Evidence Appearing Real," by Karen Armstrong, *Inside Out,* Newmarket, Ontario (in-side-out.com) October 28, 2014.

17 "SAMHSA's National Helpline is a free, confidential, 24/7, 365-day-a-year treatment referral and information service (in English and Spanish) for individuals and families facing mental and/or substance use disorders," Samhsa.gov. 1-800-662-HELP (4357).

18 "Can Lion's Roar Paralyzed Humans?" by Jamie P., Nature World News, December 17, 2020.

19 Joshua 1:9—"Have I not commanded you? Be strong and courageous. Do not be afraid; do not be discouraged, for the Lord your God will be with you wherever you go." (The Holy Bible; NIV)

20 *Switch on Your Brain*, by Dr. Caroline Leaf, page 175.

21 "Impala: A Wildlife Guide to the African Impala," safariafricana.com; "Impala: Aepyceros melampus," National Geographic. Retrieved June 12, 2020.

22 "There's a SMART Way to Write Management's Goals and Objectives," 1981, by George Doran, consultant and former director of corporate planning for Washington Water Power Company.

23 "The How-To Guide to Creating Good Habits and Breaking Bad Ones," forbes.com, March 24, 2022.

24 *The Principles and Benefits of Change: Fulfilling Your Purpose in Unsettled Times*, by Dr. Myles Munroe, page 16.

25 Ecclesiastes 3:1–8—"To everything there is a season, and a time to every purpose under the heaven: A time to be born, and a time to die; a time to plant, and a time to pluck up that which is planted;

A time to kill, and a time to heal; a time to break down, and a time to build up; A time to weep, and a time to laugh; a time to mourn, and a time to dance; A time to cast away stones, and a time to gather stones together; a time to embrace, and a time to refrain from embracing; A time to get, and a time to lose; a time to keep, and a time to cast away; A time to rend, and a time to sew; a time to keep silence, and a time to speak; A time to love, and a time to hate; a time of war, and a time of peace." (The Holy Bible; KJV)

26 Philippians 3:13–14—"Brothers and sisters, I do not consider myself yet to have taken hold of it. But one thing I do: Forgetting what is behind and straining toward what is ahead, I press on toward the goal to win the prize for which God has called me heavenward in Christ Jesus."

27 "Change Is Hard. Here's How to Make It Less Painful," by Erika Andersen, *Harvard Business Review* (hbr.org), April 7, 2022.